Educational Research and Innovation

Promoting Education Decision Makers' Use of Evidence in Austria

Florian Köster, Claire Shewbridge and Clara Krämer

This work is published under the responsibility of the Secretary-General of the OECD. The opinions expressed and arguments employed herein do not necessarily reflect the official views of OECD member countries.

This document, as well as any data and map included herein, are without prejudice to the status of or sovereignty over any territory, to the delimitation of international frontiers and boundaries and to the name of any territory, city or area.

Please cite this publication as:
Köster, F., C. Shewbridge and C. Krämer (2020), *Promoting Education Decision Makers' Use of Evidence in Austria*, Educational Research and Innovation, OECD Publishing, Paris, *https://doi.org/10.1787/0ac0181e-en*.

ISBN 978-92-64-94320-9 (print)
ISBN 978-92-64-63835-8 (pdf)

Educational Research and Innovation
ISSN 2076-9660 (print)
ISSN 2076-9679 (online)

Photo credits: Cover © Milan M/Shutterstock.com.

Corrigenda to publications may be found on line at: *www.oecd.org/about/publishing/corrigenda.htm*.
© OECD 2020

The use of this work, whether digital or print, is governed by the Terms and Conditions to be found at *http://www.oecd.org/termsandconditions*.

Foreword

Austria is committed to optimising education in its complex federal system, moving decisions closer to the students to strengthen every student's opportunity to succeed. It has undertaken great efforts in reforming its governance system and simplifying complex arrangements of responsibilities and activities. With the Education Reform Act 2017 (*Bildungsreformgesetz* 2017), it has started to reform comprehensively the governance of its school system. The reform brings together administrative responsibilities of provinces (*Länder*) and the federal level in education directorates in each of the nine provinces. School supervision adopts a regional focus over the previously functional separation between school types, and schools receive greater autonomy to cater to the needs of their students. Austria seeks to strengthen the capacity of decision makers at all levels of governance to carry out their new responsibilities.

The Federal Ministry for Education, Science and Research (BMBWF) is conscious of the importance of effective knowledge governance for the cooperation across multiple levels of governance and diverse decision makers. To this end, it seeks to strengthen the capacity of decision makers at all levels of the education system to use evidence effectively for their respective practice – including teaching and quality assurance. To address this challenge in a targeted way, the BMBWF seeks to identify what it takes to promote the systematic use of evidence and assess the respective strengths and weaknesses in current processes and opportunities available to decision makers. These efforts are accompanied by the development of a comprehensive education monitoring system to strengthen the supply of information.

OECD work on strategic education governance supports countries in identifying the best ways to achieve national objectives for education systems in a context of multi-level governance structures and complex environments. It identifies and promotes effective governance processes in the domains of accountability, capacity, knowledge governance, stakeholder involvement, strategic thinking and a whole-of-system perspective. Central to this work is an applied policy toolkit. Informed by empirical research, the toolkit's generalised questionnaires in individual domains of strategic governance help policy makers bring effective governance processes onto the political agenda. The questionnaires are adapted to individual contexts and priorities, providing countries with a set of aspirational efforts for self-reflection. They offer a common language to enable sharing of local practices and promote dialogue among stakeholders.

Part of the work on knowledge governance, the aim of this report is to take stock of processes that research finds to promote the systematic use of evidence in decision making. Carried out as an online survey to decision makers in the Austrian Federal Ministry for Education, Science and Research, education directorates, school supervision and school leaders, it is meant to gauge areas for further investigation and informing thinking about possible next practices. It is designed as a conversation starter rather than a definitive evaluation of practices. Following the spirit of a self-reflective exercise, the report informs discussions at a workshop with stakeholders of all levels of governance in the Austrian education system.

Acknowledgements

This report draws on responses to an online survey among executives at the Austrian Federal Ministry for Education, Science and Research (BMBWF), at education directorates across the nine Austrian provinces (*Länder*), and from school leaders of all school types from across Austria. Our utmost gratitude goes to all participants of this survey for taking the time to answer the questionnaire and for their efforts to provide valuable insights into their work practices and contexts.

The survey was input as an online survey software and administered by graduate students of the Vienna University of Economics and Business. We thank Jasmin Fischer, Alma Pekmezovic, Bernd Franz Pfeiffer, and Jennifer Schaden for their hard work and flexibility, as well as Professor Isabell Egger-Peitler for helpful reflections on the adapted questionnaire.

The OECD team is indebted to the Austrian Federal Ministry for Education, Science and Research (BMBWF) as partner in developing the online survey and producing the report. Our gratitude goes to Bernhard Chabera for his invaluable contributions and support making this undertaking possible, and Matthias Hansy for his dedication and tireless effort to make this enterprise a successful one throughout all its phases. We thank Michaela Jonach, Stefan Polzer, Mark Nemet and Gertrudis Spitzbart for corrections and valuable additions to the draft.

This report was prepared as part of the Strategic Education Governance project within the OECD Centre for Educational Research and Innovation. Claire Shewbridge leads the project and contributed chapter 4. Florian Köster developed the conceptual framework and generalised questionnaire, coordinated the work, and led the analysis and drafting of the report. Clara Krämer contributed to the analysis and drafting.

Our thanks go also to Glenn Fahey, previously a member of the OECD Strategic Education Governance project and now research fellow at the Centre for Independent Studies (Australia), for his valuable support in the initial development of the generalised questionnaire, and Leonora Lynch-Stein for editorial support.

The team is further grateful to Laurenz Langer, Janice Tripney, and David Gough for their research on promoting evidence use, which contributed fundamentally to the development of the framework and generalised questionnaire that underpins the analysis carried out in this report. Special thanks go to Laurenz Langer for his valuable contributions at the advisory group meeting to refine the generalised questionnaire.

Table of contents

Foreword	3
Acknowledgements	4
Executive Summary	7
1 Introduction	9
References	11
2 Strategic education governance	12
References	15
3 Knowledge governance and promoting the systematic use of evidence	17
Strengthening the skills to access and make sense of evidence	19
Making adequate evidence conveniently available	20
Organisational processes encouraging the use of evidence	20
Interaction with evidence producers and collegial exchange	21
Common understanding of fit-for-purpose evidence and how to use evidence	22
References	22
4 Evidence use in Austrian schools: International comparative data	25
A culture of shared decision making in Austrian schools	26
The evolution of quality assurance and types of evidence used	27
References	29
5 Promoting the use of evidence in Austria's education system	31
Using evidence in the federal ministry and education directorates	32
School quality managers – evidence use at the intersection of school and regional development	38
The use of evidence in schools	46
References	59
Notes	60
6 Conclusions and outlook	61
Overarching key findings	62
Relative strengths and weaknesses over five areas to promote use of evidence	63
Possible next steps	66
References	67
Note	68

Annex A. Glossary 69

FIGURES

Figure 2.1. Domains of strategic education governance	14
Figure 3.1. Promoting the systematic use of evidence in decision making	19
Figure 4.1. Monitoring teaching practices	27
Figure 4.2. Incidence of quality assurance practices in Austria compared to OECD average	28
Figure 5.1. Involving stakeholders in making evidence available in BMBWF/ education directorates	34
Figure 5.2. Involving diverse perspectives in decision making in BMBWF/ education directorates	35
Figure 5.3. Efforts by BMBWF/ education directorates raising awareness for using evidence	37
Figure 5.4. BMBWF/ education directorates developing common understanding of using evidence	38
Figure 5.5. Main evidence providers and sources of evidence used by school quality managers	41
Figure 5.6. Tasks for which school quality managers prepare evidence themselves	42
Figure 5.7. SQMs' involving of diverse perspectives in decision making and use of evidence	43
Figure 5.8. The aims of collegial exchange among school quality managers	45
Figure 5.9. SQM's efforts in the education region to develop standards of how to use evidence	45
Figure 5.10. Fostering awareness of using evidence as basis of good decision-making in schools	46
Figure 5.11. School sizes across school types	47
Figure 5.12. Barriers to use evidence expressed in school leaders' additional responses	48
Figure 5.13. Schools working with school quality managers to support use of evidence	51
Figure 5.14. Schools work with selected support offers to help them use evidence effectively	52
Figure 5.15. School's efforts to clarify decisions and how decisions are reached	54
Figure 5.16. Schools involve diverse perspectives mainly in development of classroom teaching	55
Figure 5.17. Schools' exchange with evidence providers	56
Figure 5.18. Organisational support of school's exchange with evidence providers	57
Figure 5.19. School leaders' collegial exchange on methods and experiences using evidence	58
Figure 6.1. Relative strong and weak areas to promote the systematic use of evidence	64
Figure 6.2. Overview of positive responses across areas to promote systematic use of evidence	65

TABLES

Table 4.1. Uses of student test results in Austria compared to OECD average (PISA 2015)	29
Table 5.1. Number of education regions, school quality managers and response rate by province	39
Table 5.2. School leader response rates by school type	47
Table 5.3. School leader response rates across provinces	48

Executive Summary

Introduction

The 2017 Education Reform Act in Austria gives education governance a regional focus and moves key decisions closer to schools and students. An important aspect, therefore, is to strengthen the capacity to use evidence for decisions, including in teaching and quality assurance. In support of this, Austria worked with the OECD to conduct a self-assessment exercise on evidence use among key decision makers at the federal and provincial levels (federal ministry and education directorate executives), regional level (school quality managers) and school leaders. Decision makers completed an online survey covering five areas that promote the capability, motivation, and opportunity to use evidence in decision making:

1. The skills to access and make sense of evidence.
2. Making relevant evidence conveniently available to decision makers.
3. Fostering the organisational processes and structures that encourage use of evidence.
4. Fostering the exchange among decision makers and their exchange with evidence producers and
5. Promoting use of evidence as a principle of good decision making, building a shared understanding on what constitutes fit-for-purpose evidence, as well as how and when evidence should be used.

The results and analysis in this report act as a "thermometer" gauging areas for further investigation and informing thinking about possible next practices. It is a conversation starter rather than a comparative evaluation of practices. As a first step, this report will be discussed at a workshop with representative stakeholders from each province and decision making level.

Main findings

Some provinces systematically report efforts to promote the use of evidence. In these provinces, school quality managers consistently report frequent exchanges with colleagues and evidence providers to improve evidence quality and preparation. Across schools, school leaders systematically report that they exchange with school quality managers and peers about methods and experiences working with evidence; and that these exchanges are supported organisationally, such as through requisite time or staff resources. In other provinces, such efforts are emergent.

School quality managers play a pivotal role in fostering the use of evidence. More than 90% of school quality managers report engaging in efforts to raise awareness of the merit and importance of using evidence in decision making. While such efforts focus on school leaders, six in ten school quality managers go beyond this and directly engage teaching staff. School quality managers, although largely content with the available evidence, express motivation to be more involved in preparing and providing evidence, including greater interaction with key evidence providers.

Schools are important evidence producers and have some key organisational processes in place that can encourage the use of evidence. The vast majority of school leaders report producing and using school-level evidence from internal evaluations and standardised student testing. Many school leaders highlighted concrete efforts at their schools to prepare evidence, which can provide a starting point for further dialogue and investigation. There is an emphasis on internal exchange to increase clarity around school decisions and decision-making processes. School leaders report inviting diverse perspectives, for instance from teachers, parents, and students, mainly to help develop classroom teaching.

Evidence provided to schools is not always adequately prepared for their work. Only 50% of school quality managers agree that evidence is largely or very adequate for the work of schools (regardless of the evidence provider). Compared to other evidence providers, schools report that the federal ministry and education directorates are less concerned about preparing evidence in a user-friendly way (only 41% report they are largely or very interested in doing so).

Possible next steps

Considering the changed responsibilities brought about by the 2017 Education Reform Act and building on existing efforts and available opportunities, there are a number of possible inroads for Austria to consider in its continuing efforts to promote the use of evidence.

Structuring collegial exchanges around explicit purposes, building on existing habits. Results show that interactions with peers, for both school leaders and school quality managers, are important ways of exchanging experiences and methods of evidence use. Where evidence use is not yet systematic, collegial exchanges could be structured around an explicit purpose, such as developing skills to gather, access and make sense of evidence, developing a common understanding of what makes evidence fit for a specific purpose, and developing an agreement on how evidence should be used in a specific situation. Importantly, basing such efforts on existing work habits and processes would increase their uptake and minimise administrative burden.

Increasing availability of specific training on guiding and instructing evidence use. For both school leaders and school quality managers, developing the skills to guide and instruct the use of evidence in schools is essential. Yet, reports indicate that such training is not widely available. Increasing the availability of specific training can help promote use of evidence directly and insert important new knowledge into the widely reported collegial exchanges.

Developing a common understanding around using evidence. This pertains to developing agreement around which evidence is fit-for-purpose for which tasks and how it is best used in concrete situations. This is particularly relevant in the transition to new responsibilities as specific decision-making situations and habits are still emerging.

Collaboratively reflecting on which evidence is best gathered where. While schools are important evidence producers, in some circumstances other providers, such as school quality managers, will be in a better position to gather and prepare fit-for-purpose evidence. In the same vein, schools will be in a better position to gather evidence needed at other levels. Different levels of governance – in particular, school leaders and school quality managers – should be involved in a collaborative reflection on how to optimise evidence provision.

Improving tailoring of evidence based on direct feedback from decision makers. Not all decision makers will be equally prepared to gather and prepare evidence as needed for their new responsibilities. Evidence providers need information about decision makers' work processes and habits, so that they can tailor evidence to their needs. Responses indicate that school quality managers are motivated to be directly involved in preparing evidence. Informational exchanges may be better suited for feedback on schools' needs.

1 Introduction

This section explains the motivation for the analysis in the context of governance reforms within the Austrian education system. It presents the structure of the report.

The Education Reform Act 2017 (*Bildungsreformgesetz* 2017) comprehensively reforms the governance of the Austrian school system. Its regional focus moves decisions closer to the regional environment of schools and students. Schools receive greater autonomy to cater to the needs of their students. The former system of school supervision, which was organised separately for each school type, adopts a regional focus: school quality managers are responsible for supporting schools in developing their quality based on a framework common to all school types. Additionally, the federal ministry seeks to establish a separate school evaluation body, a function previously exercised by school supervisors. The reform brings together administrative responsibilities of provinces (*Länder*) and the federal level in an education directorate in each province (BMBWF, 2019[1]).

The reform addresses the previously complex distribution of responsibilities between the federal and provincial level of governance, characterised by a fragmentation along federal and provincial schools, complexities in federal funding for teacher salaries of provincial schools, and limited autonomy of schools over staff and finances. Previous OECD analysis found these complexities to produce incentives for over- and misspending, make decision making more difficult through a lack of clarity, lead to mistrust among actors, and prevent greater integration to governing the school system (Nusche et al., 2016[2]).

An important aspect of the 2017 governance reform in Austria is to strengthen the use of evidence for decision making at all levels of governance. In an ongoing effort to strengthen the supply of data, the Federal Ministry for Education, Science and Research (*Bundesministerium für Bildung, Wissenschaft und Forschung*, BMBWF) is developing a comprehensive monitoring system, which integrates several data sources to enable access for all responsible actors in the school system. Austria observed a seeming lack of capacity to use evidence and data systematically for decision making, including in quality assurance and in teaching and learning.

To strengthen the demand-side of evidence, Austria worked with the OECD's strategic education governance team to apply its policy toolkit for promoting the systematic use of evidence by decision makers. An online survey was developed and administered among key decision makers in the federal ministry and education directorates, school quality managers and school leaders. The OECD analysis on the survey results takes stock of efforts promoting the systematic use of evidence in the Austrian education system and reflects on possible measures to strengthen them. The analysis draws on the Austrian context and current reform efforts, and is grounded in the OECD framework for strategic education governance.

Following this introduction, Section 2 introduces the OECD framework for strategic education governance, providing the background for the analysis. Section 3 discusses which efforts empirical research finds to strengthen the use of evidence in five areas: the skills to access and make sense of evidence, making evidence conveniently available, organisational processes encouraging the use of evidence, collaboration with evidence producers and collegial exchange, and building a common understanding of the importance of evidence, which evidence is useful and how it is best used. Section 4 discusses the Austrian context with a look to international comparison. Section 5 analyses the survey results, structured around policy making (BMBWF and education directorates), quality assurance (school quality managers, SQM) and schools (school leaders). The analysis of results focuses on strengths and weaknesses in the preconditions and efforts to use evidence systematically for decision making. The final section concludes and provides an outlook to possible next steps.

References

BMBWF (2019), *Steuerung des Schulsystems in Österreich: Weissbuch [Governance of the Education System in Austria: White Paper]*, Bundesministerium für Bildung, Wissenschaft und Forschung, Abt. III/3, http://www.bmbwf.gv.at. [1]

Nusche, D. et al. (2016), *OECD Reviews of School Resources: Austria 2016*, OECD Reviews of School Resources, OECD Publishing, Paris, https://dx.doi.org/10.1787/9789264256729-en. [2]

2 Strategic education governance

The section introduces the OECD framework for strategic education governance, which constitutes the background for the analysis. It provides a brief description of the six domains underpinning strategic education governance: accountability, capacity, knowledge governance, stakeholder involvement, strategic thinking and a whole-of-system perspective.

One of the most important developments in education governance has been decentralisation to enable greater responsiveness to diverse local demands. Systems are characterised by multi-level governance where the links between multiple actors operating at different levels are subject to change.

Education systems have been moving away from hierarchical relationships to a division of labour, joint activity and self-regulation. As a result, there is an increased number of actors, who need one another and whose activity increasingly takes place across rather than within organisations (Osborne, 2006[1]). Lump-sum funding, strengthening of stakeholders, horizontal accountability and holding local authorities and schools accountable through performance indicators have changed the nature of the relationship between the national and subnational levels (provinces and regions, intermediate governments and municipalities). With joint provision and collaborative activity, actors may 'wear a range of hats', which can make it difficult to discern who is accountable for what, when, and to whom (Romzek, 2011[2]).

At the same time, parents and other stakeholders join government authorities in education decision making. Relationships between stakeholders and decision makers are increasingly dynamic and open to negotiation. The various actors, such as policy makers at various levels, parents, and teachers, have varying perspectives on problems. Interpretations of the reality differ, and so do expectations and preferred solutions. Information is now more widely gathered than ever before, and while the growing availability of information allows new insights and approaches to shape education, it also prompts new demands and uncertainties.

Ministries of education nevertheless remain responsible for ensuring high quality, efficient, equitable and innovative education at the national level. OECD research identified six interdependent domains of strategic education governance to help government authorities manage the dynamism and complexity of today's education systems while steering a clear course towards established goals. Conditioning each other, these six domain are accountability, capacity, knowledge governance, stakeholder involvement, strategic thinking and a whole-of-system perspective (Figure 2.1).

Accountability pertains to organising who renders an account to whom and for what an account is rendered, and shaping incentives and disincentives for behaviour. In context of reduced hierarchical control and diverse local challenges and contexts, local discretion is central to respond to students' and other stakeholders' diverse needs. At the same time, limiting fragmentation helps to improve learning from each other and pursuing common goals (Blanchenay and Burns, 2016[3]; Burns, Köster and Fuster, 2016[4]). Accountability plays a central role in providing the space and incentives to learn and improve practice (Köster and Krämer, forthcoming[5]).

The domain of **capacity** pertains to ensuring decision makers, organisations and systems have the adequate resources and capabilities to fulfil their roles and tasks. Resources pertain to financial and human resources, as well as time and material resources, such as technical equipment. The distribution of responsibilities and knowledge across governance levels and diverse local contexts create specific concerns around ensuring capacity. This pertains centrally to capacity for policy making at sub-central levels of governance and capacity for implementation and evaluation (Blanchenay and Burns, 2016[3]). In addition, diverse local contexts and stakeholders with distinct capacity legacies render centrally identifying needs and building capacity inefficient. Horizontal and collaborative approaches to building capacity promise efficiency gains (Burns, Köster and Fuster, 2016[4]).

Knowledge governance pertains to stimulating the production of relevant knowledge and promoting its use in decision making. Knowledge governance takes an important role in enabling actors to respond to developments, align their activities, learn and improve practice, and identify and address individual, organisational and systemic capacity gaps. This relates to producing adequate and comprehensive evidence, mobilising evidence for convenient use, stimulating a culture of evidence use, and nurturing evidence-related capabilities (Langer, Tripney and Gough, 2016[6]; Hess and Ostrom, 2007[7]).

Figure 2.1. Domains of strategic education governance

Accountability
- Enabling local discretion while limiting fragmentation
- Promoting a culture of learning and improvement

Capacity
- Ensuring capacity for policy-making and implementation
- Stimulating horizontal capacity building

Knowledge governance
- Promoting production of adequate evidence
- Mobilising produced evidence for convenient use
- Stimulating a culture of evidence-use
- Nurturing evidence-related capabilities

Stakeholder involvement
- Integrating stakeholder knowledge and perspectives
- Fostering support, shared responsibility, ownership and trust

Strategic thinking
- Crafting, sharing and consolidating a system vision
- Adapting to changing contexts and new knowledge
- Balancing short-term and long-term priorities

Whole-of-system perspective
- Overcoming system inertia
- Developing synergies within the system and moderating tensions

Source: Shewbridge and Köster (2019[8]) *Strategic Education Governance - Project Plan and Organisational Framework*, http://www.oecd.org/education/ceri/SEG-Project-Plan-org-framework.pdf

Stakeholder involvement pertains to involving the perspectives and demands of stakeholders effectively and efficiently in policy and governance. With less direct hierarchical control, decentralised decision making and knowledge, and greater influence of stakeholders, policy requires support of a wide range of stakeholders. Integrating stakeholders' knowledge and perspectives is central in adapting policies to local contexts, legacies and demands. Engaging stakeholders can foster sustainable change by promoting ownership, trust, and mobilising legitimacy for policy (Colgan, Rochford and Burke, 2016[9]; Pierre and Peters, 2005[10]).

Strategic thinking pertains to balancing short-term priorities with long-term perspectives, and adapting strategies to new knowledge. Education governance faces changing contexts, new knowledge emerges from a broad range of sources, and demands and preferences change. In consequence, effective policy strategies emerge and evolve (Mason, 2016[11]; Snyder, 2013[12]). With diverse stakeholders involved in governance, decentralised responsibilities and distributed knowledge, policy making requires strategic thinking and requisite capacity at all levels of the system. Strategic thinking includes building a common vision for the education system that incorporates various perspectives of stakeholders across the system. It includes practices to adapt strategies and goals as contexts change and new knowledge emerges and to coordinate action and balancing tensions (Frankowski et al., 2018[13]; Burns and Köster, 2016[14]; OECD, 2019[15]; Burns, Köster and Fuster, 2016[4]).

Adopting a **whole-of-system perspective** pertains to adopting perspectives reaching beyond individual realms of responsibility to coordinate across decision makers, governance levels and policies. With often informal interdependence and collaborative activity, isolated interventions may prompt adverse effects elsewhere in the system; synergies between various parts of the system may not be realised; and fragmentation of policy approaches can produce inefficiencies (Colgan, Rochford and Burke, 2016[9]). A whole-of-system perspective seeks to align policies, stakeholders' roles and responsibilities across the system. It can help moderating tensions between priorities – e.g. risk-avoidance and innovation, consensus building and making difficult choices – and identifying and developing synergies (Burns, Köster and Fuster, 2016[4]). Communicating the successes of a whole-of-system perspective can help establish legitimacy and mobilise stakeholder support for collaborative approaches (Colgan, Rochford and Burke, 2016[9]).

References

Blanchenay, P. and T. Burns (2016), "Policy experimentation in complex education systems", in Burns, T. and F. Köster (eds.), *Governing Education in a Complex World*, OECD Publishing, Paris, http://dx.doi.org/10.1787/9789264255364-10-en. [3]

Burns, T. and F. Köster (eds.) (2016), *Governing Education in a Complex World*, Educational Research and Innovation, OECD Publishing, Paris, https://dx.doi.org/10.1787/9789264255364-en. [14]

Burns, T., F. Köster and M. Fuster (2016), *Education Governance in Action: Lessons from Case Studies*, Educational Research and Innovation, OECD Publishing, Paris, https://dx.doi.org/10.1787/9789264262829-en. [4]

Colgan, A., S. Rochford and K. Burke (2016), *Implementing public service reform Messages from the literature*, Centre for Effective Services, Dublin, http://www.effectiveservices.org (accessed on 5 October 2017). [9]

Frankowski, A. et al. (2018), "Dilemmas of central governance and distributed autonomy in education", *OECD Education Working Papers*, No. 189, OECD Publishing, Paris, https://dx.doi.org/10.1787/060260bf-en. [13]

Hess, C. and E. Ostrom (eds.) (2007), *Understanding Knowledge as a Commons - From Theory to Practice*, MIT Press, Cambridge, London, http://mitpress.mit.edu. [7]

Köster, F. and C. Krämer (forthcoming), "A practical framework for meaningful accountability in education (working title)", *OECD Education Working Papers*, OECD Publishing, Paris. [5]

Langer, L., J. Tripney and D. Gough (2016), *The Science of Using Science - Researching the Use of Research Evidence in Decision-Making*, EPPI-Centre, Social Science Research Unit, UCL Institute of Education, University College London, http://eppi.ioe.ac.uk/cms/Default. (accessed on 15 January 2018). [6]

Mason, M. (2016), "Complexity theory and systemic change in education governance", in Burns, T. and F. Köster (eds.), *Governing Education in a Complex World*, OECD Publishing, Paris, http://dx.doi.org/10.1787/9789264255364-4-en. [11]

OECD (2019), *Improving School Quality in Norway: The New Competence Development Model*, Implementing Education Policies, OECD Publishing, Paris, https://dx.doi.org/10.1787/179d4ded-en. [15]

Osborne, S. (2006), "The New Public Governance?", *Public Management Review*, Vol. 8/3, pp. 377-387, http://dx.doi.org/10.1080/14719030600853022. [1]

Pierre, J. and B. Peters (2005), *Governing Complex Societies: Trajectories and Scenarios*, Palgrave Macmillan, Nw York. [10]

Romzek, B. (2011), "The tangled web of accountability in contracting networks: The case of welfare reform", in Dubnick, M. and H. Frederickson (eds.), *Accountable Government : Problems and Promises*, Routledge, http://ebookcentral.proquest.com/lib/uts/detail.action?docID=1900108. [2]

Shewbridge, C. and F. Köster (2019), *Strategic Education Governance - Project Plan and Organisational Framework*, http://www.oecd.org/education/ceri/SEG-Project-Plan-org-framework.pdf. [8]

Snyder, S. (2013), "The simple, the complicated, and the complex: Educational reform through the lens of complexity theory", *OECD Education Working Papers*, No. 96, OECD Publishing, Paris, http://dx.doi.org/10.1787/5k3txnpt1lnr-en. [12]

3 Knowledge governance and promoting the systematic use of evidence

The section describes efforts that empirical research finds to strengthen the decision makers systematic use of evidence. The section discusses efforts in five areas: 1) the skills to access and make sense of evidence; 2) making evidence conveniently available; 3) fostering organisational processes and structures that encourage evidence use; 4) fostering the exchange among decision makers and their exchange with evidence producers; and 5) building standards related to using evidence.

The complexity of education systems requires particular attention to knowledge processes. Data and other information relevant for decision making is collected and needed at potentially different times and places. It is often produced in some form and needed in another to inform decision making. Actors have diverse responsibilities and roles and may produce some information and require other in their decision-making processes (Burns, Köster and Fuster, 2016[1]).

On the supply side, knowledge governance means bringing together varied, adequate and relevant information and knowledge. This includes producing knowledge directly, for example through policy experimentation, piloting and evaluation, as well as collecting and consolidating administrative and performance data. It includes facilitating knowledge production, for example by shaping funding channels or otherwise incentivising research activities and evidence production (Langer, Tripney and Gough, 2016[2]). For information to be useful for decision making in policy and practice, decision makers need to transform information into actionable knowledge. Knowledge pertains to "assimilated information and the understanding of how to use it" (Hess and Ostrom, 2007, p. 8[3]).

Decisions in professional and policy-making contexts draw on a wide range of knowledge and complex considerations so that evidence cannot be the only factor driving decisions. Policy decisions are embedded in value-driven political context and may have no or multiple technically 'best' solutions (Newman and Head, 2017[4]). Teachers' and other professionals' decisions in classrooms and workplaces are directed by a vast amount of practical and tacit knowledge. This allows decision makers to adapt to local contexts and puts them in the best position to identify the sources of evidence, data and other information necessary for the specific decision-making challenge at hand. However, decision makers may also lack the opportunity or motivation to integrate new information into their knowledge or to move beyond familiar approaches. They may lack the capability to do so effectively and efficiently. They may follow beliefs about what works or engage in cognitive shortcuts (heuristics) rather than drawing on systematic investigation to gather adequate evidence and decide on a course of action in a given context (Fahey and Köster, 2019[5]; Burns, Köster and Fuster, 2016[1]).

In the context of this complexity, the demand side of knowledge governance means promoting decision makers' capability, motivation, and opportunity to consider evidence systematically when making decisions. Using evidence systematically means considering evidence beyond where it may align with preconceived notions or in specific situations.

Evidence pertains to the product of any "systematic investigative process employed to increase or revise current knowledge" (Langer, Tripney and Gough, 2016, p. 11[2]). This includes formal research, for example as carried out by research institutions, government agencies or think tanks; systematically gathered understandings from education practice and the practice of policy making, implementation, and evaluation; as well as factual administrative and achievement data (Langer, Tripney and Gough, 2016[2]).

Motivation, capability and opportunity are all needed to make use of evidence to produce actionable knowledge. Decision makers will not use evidence if they are not motivated to do so; they will not do so if they do not know how; and they will not consider evidence in their decisions when they do not have the opportunity to do so. Conversely, the three components can promote one another. For instance, the opportunity or the capability to use evidence can strengthen the motivation to do so. Moreover, using evidence successfully for a decision can expand knowledge to engage meaningfully with evidence and can motivate a more systematic use of evidence. Capability pertains to the necessary knowledge and skills to engage in the use of evidence. Motivation includes the habits as well as active decisions to use evidence. Opportunity refers to all external factors that make evidence use possible or prompt it, such as the access to a data warehouse to explore evidence and the time to do so (Michie, van Stralen and West, 2011[6]). Based on empirically observed mechanisms (Langer, Tripney and Gough, 2016[2]), the OECD Strategic Education Governance project identifies five areas to promote the capability, motivation, and opportunity to use evidence in decision making (Michie, van Stralen and West, 2011[6]). These areas pertain to: the skills to access and makes sense of evidence, making evidence conveniently available, organisational processes encouraging the use of evidence, collaboration with evidence producers and collegial exchange, and building a common understanding of the importance of evidence, which evidence is useful and how its best used (Figure 3.1).

Figure 3.1. Promoting the systematic use of evidence in decision making

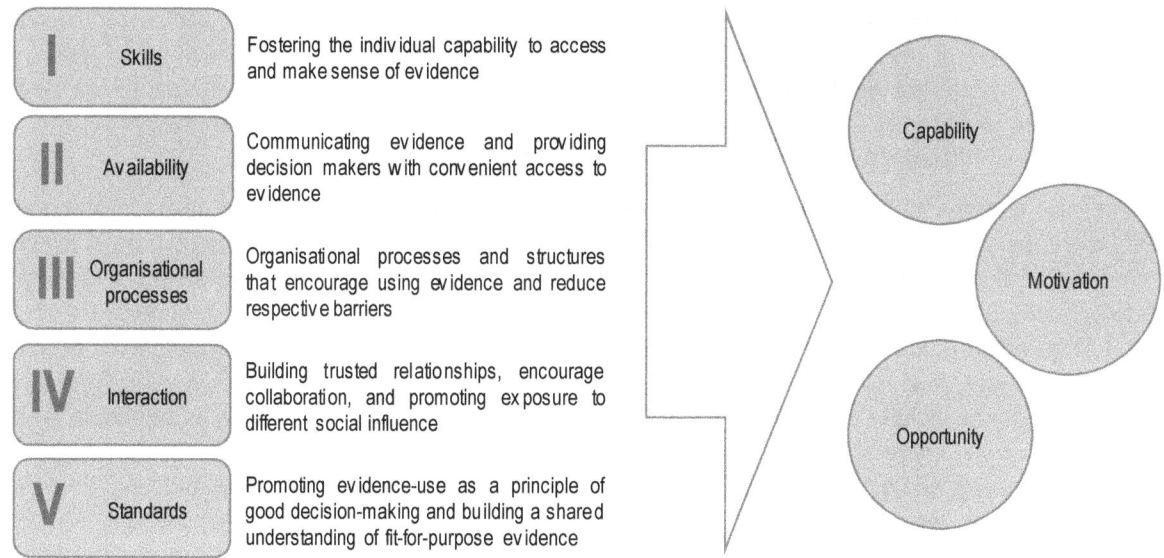

Source: Adapted from Langer, Tripney and Gough (2016[2]) The Science of Using Science – Researching the Use of Research Evidence in Decision-Making.

Strengthening the skills to access and make sense of evidence

The more proficient decision makers are in using evidence the more likely they are to use it systematically and to greater effect, as well as comprehend this evidence better in practice. Building skills for using evidence pertains to fostering the individual capability to access and make sense of evidence. This includes the skills for locating, appraising, and synthesising evidence to integrate it with other information and particular needs. Appraising evidence pertains to examining research systematically and critically, with the aim to judge its trustworthiness and its value and relevance in particular contexts (Langer, Tripney and Gough, 2016[2]; Hyde et al., 2000[7]).

Inroads to foster such skills pertain to initial education, dedicated professional training offers and other continuing education formats. This includes external offers. External training includes university courses (individual and degree), university and professional accreditations, and short courses offered by other providers. Requisite skills may be fostered also through mentoring and coaching efforts, structured exchange among colleagues, and learning platforms/ e-learning offers (Abdullah et al., 2014[8]; Chambers et al., 2011[9]). Supervisors with the skills to supervise their staff's use of evidence are more likely to motivate staff to make better use of evidence and to acquire relevant skills. This includes dedicated training offers for supervisors, continuing education formats (including external offers), mentoring/ coaching, exchange with colleagues, and learning platforms/ e-learning. To supervise effectively the use of evidence by their staff, supervisors need suitable resources comprising relevant physical and organisational resources and requisite time. Specific resources include education and training requirements, instructions/ assistance for conducting employee reviews or reflection and planning discussions, and staff development measures (Langer, Tripney and Gough, 2016[2]; Gray et al., 2012[10]).

Making adequate evidence conveniently available

Making evidence available pertains to communicating evidence and providing decision makers with convenient access to evidence. Making evidence available effectively increases the usefulness of evidence and makes evidence more likely to be used in decision making. Evidence can be communicated directly, for example through newsletters, publications, handouts, research teasers or research summaries (Cordingley, 2016[11]). Making evidence available also includes providing access to evidence, for instance through databases or evidence repositories. Databases may contain various information such as administrative or performance data and may connect these data within or across organisations. Evidence repositories are collections of consolidated evidence compiled centrally, often online, providing an organised body of related information (Langer, Tripney and Gough, 2016[2]).

Indiscriminate communication of evidence can be inefficient because it is difficult for decision makers to identify the most relevant elements for their practice. Targeting evidence to those to whom it is most relevant avoids burdening decision makers. For instance, relevant target groups at the school level may include school leaders, administrators, staff in the area of quality development, and teachers. Evidence may be targeted to students and parents as well. Within target groups, tailoring evidence to decision makers' preferences and work habits increases convenience and personal salience. Relevant dimensions for tailoring evidence include differences in experience and capabilities in dealing with evidence, interests in content/ topics, language style and proficiency, and preferred information channels such as newsletters, handouts, databases, and evidence repositories. Approaches that can be used to target and tailor evidence include consulting experts when designing knowledge resources and communication strategies; feedback discussions with users, surveys among decision makers regarding preferences and needs; consulting prospective users when designing knowledge resources; and collaborating with decision makers in making evidence available (Noar, Benac and Harris, 2007[12]; Kreuter and Wray, 2003[13]; Langer, Tripney and Gough, 2016[2]).

Collaborating with decision makers in making evidence available allows shaping communication techniques, modes of access and presentation of evidence in a manner that is most relevant for their needs. It can further help building ownership of evidence and foster future appetite for closer commitment with evidence production. Respective efforts should be mindful of time, effort and commitment required to avoid overburdening decision makers. Collaborating with decision makers includes collaboration in developing content, soliciting content (such as contributing texts), and involvement in evaluating communication techniques, tools and knowledge resources (O'Mara-Eves et al., 2013[14]; Langer, Tripney and Gough, 2016[2]).

Organisational processes encouraging the use of evidence

Organisational processes encourage and support evidence use. This includes integrating evidence use in existing processes and structures, making decision-making processes transparent and comprehensible, inviting diverse perspectives into decision making, and establishing knowledge management systems.

Use of evidence should become a routine and fluent practice. Efforts to strengthen the use of evidence should be integrated into existing decision-making processes to maximise the opportunity to use evidence directly when the need arises and motivate decision makers to use available evidence. Conversely, introducing additional structures can be ineffective where they do not fit existing processes and habits, such as introducing a knowledge broker in an environment where evidence use is already high. Shaping organisational processes and structures should include considering opportunity costs in terms of required (prior) investments in time, resources, and skills of decision makers. To promote take-up and sustainability of efforts to promote evidence use, opportunity costs should be proportional to the benefits associated with the efforts. Incremental changes in decision-making processes and structures may be more cost-effective and sustainable than more ambitious alternatives (Bunn and Sworn, 2011[15]; Langer, Tripney and Gough, 2016[2]).

Transparent and comprehensible decision-making processes make clear how decisions were reached and the assumptions made and evidence used in doing so. Highlighting how and which evidence has been considered in a given decision motivates the use of evidence. Specific tools include (publicly) accessible documents and exchange formats that discuss decisions and how they were reached. Exchanges may be among internal stakeholders, for example among the school leadership team. Exchanges may also be with external stakeholders such as the school inspectorate engaging in exchange with schools or the school exchanging with school partners (Harvey et al., 2002[16]; Nutley, Walter and Davies, 2007[17]).

Inviting a range of perspectives, experiences, and knowledge into decision-making processes can strengthen systematic use of evidence by motivating consideration of different sources of evidence. Embedding organisational instruments into efforts to enhance transparency of decisions and invite diversity in decision making is relevant to support these processes. In particular, this support can come in the form of tangible means such as procedures, protocols, or other tools employed within an organisation (Durand et al., 2014[18]).

Knowledge management serves to identify, store and link existing knowledge and to create new knowledge so that decision makers can use knowledge in a goal-oriented way. Knowledge management is relevant to support evidence use and decision making by providing links between evidence and other existing knowledge. Organisational knowledge management should align with decision-making processes to make the best possible use. Knowledge management can be online, such as online platforms and databases, as well as offline, for instance in the form of a local collection of printed handbooks, teaching materials, or organisational documents. Knowledge management can be organisation-wide or provide access to knowledge across multiple organisations, such as schools, school clusters, or education regions (Quinn et al., 2014[19]).

Interaction with evidence producers and collegial exchange

The exchange between decision makers and providers of evidence and the exchange between decision makers among themselves can provide important impulses to promote the systematic use of evidence (Kothari, Birch and Charles, 2005[20]). Interaction between evidence providers and decision makers can facilitate reaching common understanding of evidence and help evidence providers to gather information on the expectations placed on evidence by decision makers. It can motivate decision makers' use of evidence through social influence and promote the ease of use by helping decision makers understand provided evidence and understanding how to integrate it in professional processes (Langer, Tripney and Gough, 2016[2]; Kim et al., 2015[21]; Nutley, Walter and Davies, 2007[17]).

Interaction between decision makers can facilitate learning from each other and contribute to building professional standards of what fit-for-purpose evidence looks like. For example, decision makers may engage in regular meetings to discuss research in scientific journals and their application in respective professional practice ("journal club") (Harris et al., 2010[22]). Interaction among decision makers may also be targeted to develop a common understanding of how evidence should be used in specific decision making situations. For instance, this can take the form of professionals engaging in shared learning of new or better ways of undertaking practice and how evidence fits into these processes ("joint practice development") (Hargreaves, 2011[23]; Sebba, Kent and Tregenza, 2012[24]).

Three approaches promise to strengthen the potential of interaction to support evidence use apply to both interaction among decision makers and to exchange and collaboration of decision makers with evidence providers. First, interaction should be structured around an explicit purpose. This includes organising structured events like workshops and providing structured time for interaction within the organisation, for example within network meetings. Second, interaction should favour more frequent, relatively low-threshold efforts over relatively fewer, more ambitious efforts. Low-threshold exchanges offer lower potential for frictions and may be timelier by offering an opportunity to contribute to current decision-making challenges. This includes informal regular exchanges between peers, for example integrated in regular work meetings, or mentoring or coaching relationships. Third, approaches should minimise opportunity costs by supporting exchanges. This includes providing the time and opportunity to engage with evidence providers and with peers, such as through organising replacement for the decision makers in their regular responsibilities to free their time (Shippee et al., 2013[25]; Langer, Tripney and Gough, 2016[2]; O'Mara-Eves et al., 2013[14]).

Common understanding of fit-for-purpose evidence and how to use evidence

This area entails promoting use of evidence as a principle of good decision making, developing a common understanding of what constitutes fit-for-purpose evidence and how evidence should be used for specific decision-making challenges. Recognising evidence use as a principle of good decision making underpins much of the demand for evidence. The aim is to stimulate behaviour and establish a positive attitude towards using evidence in daily practice. Raising awareness entails promoting visibility of the issue and educating decision makers about the importance and the benefits of using evidence. This may include events and awareness initiatives, providing consulting services, and raising awareness within regular work meetings. It also includes providing guidance and assistance on how to raise awareness, for example through information material available to school leaders (Johnson and May, 2015[26]; Langer, Tripney and Gough, 2016[2]).

Promoting agreement on what constitutes fit-for-purpose evidence entails developing a common understanding of the requirements on evidence for it to be useful for particular decisions and challenges. An agreement on what constitutes fit-for-purpose evidence can increase efficiency of using evidence and support efficient exchanges between evidence providers and decision makers. Formalising consensus on fit-for-purpose evidence can bolster the commitment to the standards and expectations when, where and how the evidence should be used (Diamond et al., 2014[27]).

Developing common understanding of how evidence should be used increases efficiency of using evidence in decision-making and promotes systematic use of evidence. In policy making, this includes developing how evidence should be used and which role it should take in preparing, implementing and evaluating measures. In schools, standards for evidence use may pertain to school development, curriculum development, as well as using evidence in staff development decisions or for organisational measures (Paine Cronin and Sadan, 2015[28]).

References

Abdullah, G. et al. (2014), "Measuring the effectiveness of mentoring as a knowledge translation intervention for implementing empirical evidence: A systematic review", *Worldviews on Evidence-Based Nursing*, Vol. 11/5, pp. 284-300, http://dx.doi.org/10.1111/wvn.12060. [8]

Bunn, F. and K. Sworn (2011), "Strategies to promote the impact of systematic reviews on healthcare policy: A systematic review of the literature", *Evidence & Policy: A Journal of Research, Debate and Practice*, Vol. 7/4, pp. 403-428, http://dx.doi.org/10.1332/174426411X603434. [15]

Burns, T., F. Köster and M. Fuster (2016), *Education Governance in Action: Lessons from Case Studies*, Educational Research and Innovation, OECD Publishing, Paris, https://dx.doi.org/10.1787/9789264262829-en. [1]

Chambers, D. et al. (2011), "Maximizing the impact of systematic reviews in health care decision making: A systematic review of knowledge-translation resources", *The Milbank Quarterly*, Vol. 89/1, pp. 131-156. [9]

Cordingley, P. (2016), "Knowledge and research use in local capacity building", in *Governing Education in a Complex World*, OECD Publishing, Paris, https://dx.doi.org/10.1787/9789264255364-9-en. [11]

Diamond, I. et al. (2014), "Defining consensus: A systematic review recommends methodologic criteria for reporting of Delphi studies", *Journal of Clinical Epidemiology*, Vol. 67/4, pp. 401-409, http://dx.doi.org/10.1016/j.jclinepi.2013.12.002. [27]

Fahey, G. and F. Köster (2019), "Means, ends and meaning in accountability for strategic education governance", *OECD Education Working Papers*, No. 204, OECD Publishing, Paris, https://dx.doi.org/10.1787/1d516b5c-en. [5]

Gray, M. et al. (2012), "Implementing evidence-based practice", *Research on Social Work Practice*, Vol. 23/2, pp. 157-166, http://dx.doi.org/10.1177/1049731512467072. [10]

Hargreaves, D. (2011), *Leading a self-improving school system*, https://assets.publishing.service.gov.uk/government/uploads/system/uploads/attachment_data/file/325890/leading-a-self-improving-school-system.pdf. [23]

Harris, J. et al. (2010), "Are journal clubs effective in supporting evidence-based decision making? A systematic review, BEME Guide No. 16.", *Medical Teacher*, Vol. 33/1, pp. 9-23, http://dx.doi.org/10.3109/0142159x.2011.530321. [22]

Harvey, G. et al. (2002), "Getting evidence into practice: The role and function of facilitation", *Journal of Advanced Nursing*, Vol. 37/6, pp. 577-588, http://dx.doi.org/10.1046/j.1365-2648.2002.02126.x. [16]

Hess, C. and E. Ostrom (eds.) (2007), *Understanding Knowledge as a Commons - From Theory to Practice*, MIT Press, Cambridge, London, http://mitpress.mit.edu. [3]

Hyde, C. et al. (2000), *Systematic Review of Effectiveness of Teaching Critical Appraisal*, ICRF/NHS Centre for Statistics in Medicine, Institute of Health Sciences. [7]

Johnson, M. and C. May (2015), "Promoting professional behaviour change in healthcare: What interventions work, and why? A theory-led overview of systematic reviews", *BMJ Open*, Vol. 5/9, p. e008592, http://dx.doi.org/10.1136/bmjopen-2015-008592. [26]

Kim, D. et al. (2015), "Social network targeting to maximise population behaviour change: A cluster randomised controlled trial", *The Lancet*, Vol. 386/9989, pp. 145-153, http://dx.doi.org/10.1016/S0140-6736(15)60095-2. [21]

Kothari, A., S. Birch and C. Charles (2005), ""Interaction" and research utilisation in health policies and programs: does it work?", *Health Policy*, Vol. 71/1, pp. 117-125, http://dx.doi.org/10.1016/j.healthpol.2004.03.010. [20]

Kreuter, M. and R. Wray (2003), "Tailored and targeted health communication: Strategies for enhancing information relevance", *American Journal of Health Behavior*, Vol. 27/1, pp. 227-232, http://dx.doi.org/10.5993/ajhb.27.1.s3.6. [13]

Langer, L., J. Tripney and D. Gough (2016), *The Science of Using Science - Researching the Use of Research Evidence in Decision-Making*, EPPI-Centre, Social Science Research Unit, UCL Institute of Education, University College London, http://eppi.ioe.ac.uk/cms/Default. (accessed on 15 January 2018). [2]

Malaga, G. (ed.) (2014), "Do interventions designed to support shared decision-making reduce health inequalities? A systematic review and meta-analysis", *PLoS ONE*, Vol. 9/4, p. e94670, http://dx.doi.org/10.1371/journal.pone.0094670. [18]

Michie, S., M. van Stralen and R. West (2011), "The behaviour change wheel: A new method for characterising and designing behaviour change interventions", http://dx.doi.org/10.1186/1748-5908-6-42. [6]

Newman, J. and B. Head (2017), "Wicked tendencies in policy problems: Rethinking the distinction between social and technical problems", *Policy and Society*, http://dx.doi.org/10.1080/14494035.2017.1361635. [4]

Noar, S., C. Benac and M. Harris (2007), "Does tailoring matter? Meta-analytic review of tailored print health behavior change interventions.", *Psychological Bulletin*, Vol. 133/4, pp. 673-693, http://dx.doi.org/10.1037/0033-2909.133.4.673. [12]

Nutley, S., I. Walter and H. Davies (2007), *Using Evidence: How Research Informs Public Services*, Policy Press, Bristol, UK. [17]

O'Mara-Eves, A. et al. (2013), "Community engagement to reduce inequalities in health: A systematic review, meta-analysis and economic analysis", *Public Health Research*, Vol. 1/4, pp. 1-526, http://dx.doi.org/10.3310/phr01040. [14]

Paine Cronin, G. and M. Sadan (2015), "Use of evidence in policy making in South Africa: An exploratory study of attitudes of senior government officials", *African Evaluation Journal*, Vol. 3/1, http://dx.doi.org/10.4102/aej.v3i1.145. [28]

Quinn, E. et al. (2014), "How can knowledge exchange portals assist in knowledge management for evidence-informed decision making in public health?", *BMC Public Health*, Vol. 14/1, http://dx.doi.org/10.1186/1471-2458-14-443. [19]

Sebba, J., P. Kent and J. Tregenza (2012), *What Does the Evidence Suggest are Effective Approaches? Schools and Academies Resource*, http://www.badscience.net/. [24]

Shippee, N. et al. (2013), "Patient and service user engagement in research: A systematic review and synthesized framework", *Health Expectations*, Vol. 18/5, pp. 1151-1166, http://dx.doi.org/10.1111/hex.12090. [25]

4 Evidence use in Austrian schools: International comparative data

This section discusses the Austrian context in international comparison. It draws on data about decision-making culture and changed responsibilities in schools and discusses the evolution of quality assurance compared to other OECD countries.

There have been significant changes in official responsibilities for key decisions in the Austrian school system. Ten years ago, Austrian schools enjoyed less autonomy, compared to other OECD countries, with the majority of key decisions taken at the federal or provincial levels (OECD, 2012[1]).

Data collected from school leaders in PISA 2015 highlighted the comparatively lower levels of autonomy in Austrian schools. Compared to the OECD average, decision making was more centralised, with the federal government having more responsibility for teacher salaries, formulating school budgets and deciding the offer and content of courses, while the provinces had more responsibility for selecting and firing teachers (OECD, 2016[2]). However, there were notable exceptions where Austrian schools enjoyed comparatively greater autonomy. This included deciding on budget allocations within the school, establishing student assessment policies, and approving students for admission to the school.

With changes introduced in 2017, OECD administrative data indicate that Austrian schools now enjoy comparatively more responsibility for key decisions than in the OECD on average (OECD, 2018[3]). A major new school responsibility is the selection of teachers, as well as conducting training and further education planning discussions. Schools can make decisions on teacher professional development in full autonomy. Other autonomy gains include opening times, class numbers and flexible organisation of lesson times (BMBWF, 2019[4]). These increased responsibilities have important implications for Austrian school leaders. To promote a common understanding of school management, an official profile was established as part of the 2017 reform. This can serve as a basis for the development of initial and further education programmes and also for school quality managers in their work in supervising and supporting school quality. The essential school management tasks are (BMBWF, 2019[4]):

- strategic orientation of school education
- continuous development of teaching
- establishment of structures and process design
- personnel and material resources management
- selection of teachers
- staff development for teachers
- management of administrative and support staff
- internal and external communication
- conflict and crisis management
- self-reflection and self-development.

A culture of shared decision making in Austrian schools

Austrian teachers play a lead role in many school-level decisions (OECD, 2020[5]). In 2018, a comparatively high proportion of Austrian lower secondary teachers (83%, compared to the OECD average 77%) report that they have opportunities to actively participate in school decisions. Among lower secondary schools with management teams, the vast majority of Austrian school leaders report that teachers are represented on the team. In fact, 70% report that teachers have significant responsibility in a majority of tasks related to school policies, curriculum and instruction. Regarding one of the newer areas of school autonomy, 81% of Austrian lower secondary teachers report that they have control over determining course content (compared to an OECD average of 84%) (OECD, 2020[5]).

In 2008, the New Secondary School Reform (*Neue Mittelschule*, NMS) introduced new roles for teachers, including subject coordinators and school development teams. New Secondary Schools (NMS) have since replaced the previous General Secondary Schools (Hauptschule, HS) and new roles for teachers have been comprehensively adopted. The 2008 reform also introduced resources for team teaching in a single classroom (Nusche et al., 2016[6]). This hoped to stimulate a more collaborative working culture and appears to have had some success: In 2018 Austrian lower secondary teachers report high levels of collegiality and indeed greater professional collaboration and exchange and co-ordination for teaching compared to the OECD average (OECD, 2020[5]).

The evolution of quality assurance and types of evidence used

In 2015, Austrian school leader reports indicate that several quality assurance practices were less prominent in Austrian schools than in the OECD on average (OECD, 2016[2]). These include practices to promote more coherence in teaching and learning, including written specification of the school's curricular profile, educational goals and student performance standards. Around half of Austrian school leaders reported that their school had not implemented a standardised policy for reading subjects in 2018, similar to reports in 2015 regarding science subjects. Austrian lower secondary teachers also report comparatively less coherent beliefs among staff about teaching and learning in 2018 (61% in Austria, 76% in the OECD on average) (OECD, 2020[5]).

Figure 4.1. Monitoring teaching practices

Percentage of students in schools where the school leader reported this practice in PISA

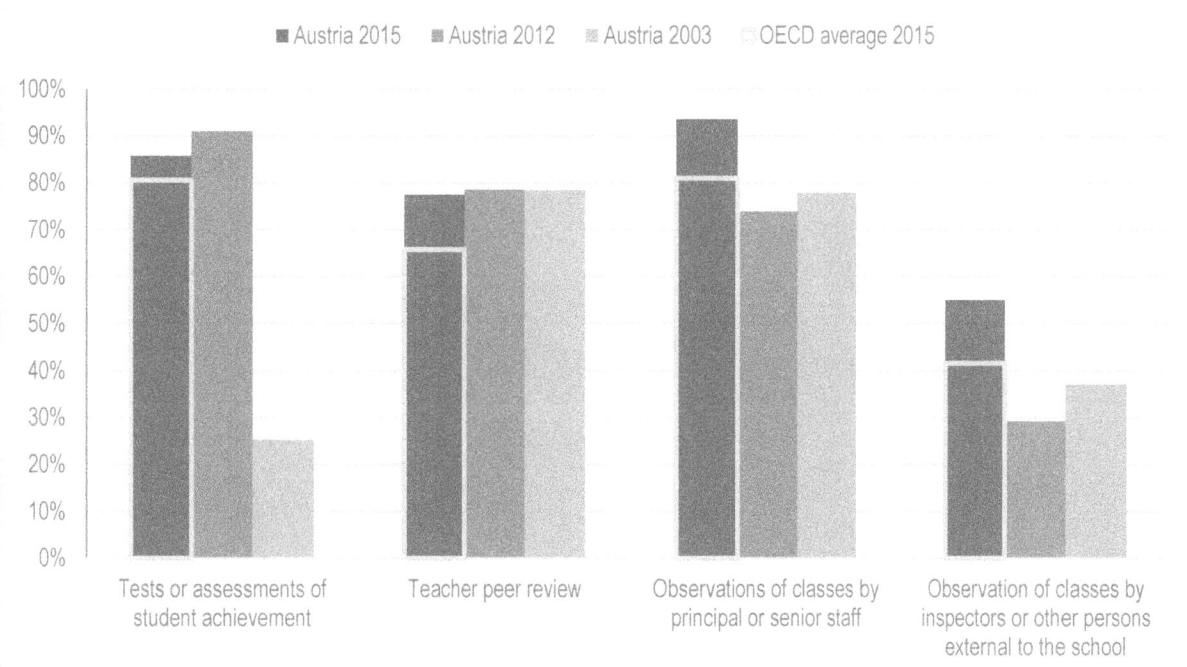

Note: In 2015, school leaders were asked about practices to monitor teachers at their school; in 2003 and 2012 the same question related to mathematics teachers.
Source: Compiled from data in (OECD, 2016[2]) PISA 2015 Results (Volume II): Policies and Practices for Successful Schools

Although external evaluation is comparatively less prominent in Austrian lower secondary schools, school principals report initiatives to gather evidence from other sources. Regular consultation with experts for school improvement and seeking feedback from students is more prominent in Austrian schools than in the OECD on average, according to school leader reports in 2015 (Figure 4.2).In a similar vein, Austrian school leader reports indicate use of a broad set of evidence for monitoring teaching practices, including the observation of classes by the school leader, senior staff, inspectors or other external experts and teacher peer review (Figure 4.1).

Figure 4.2. Incidence of quality assurance practices in Austria compared to OECD average

Percentage of students in schools where the school principal reported the following actions (PISA 2015)

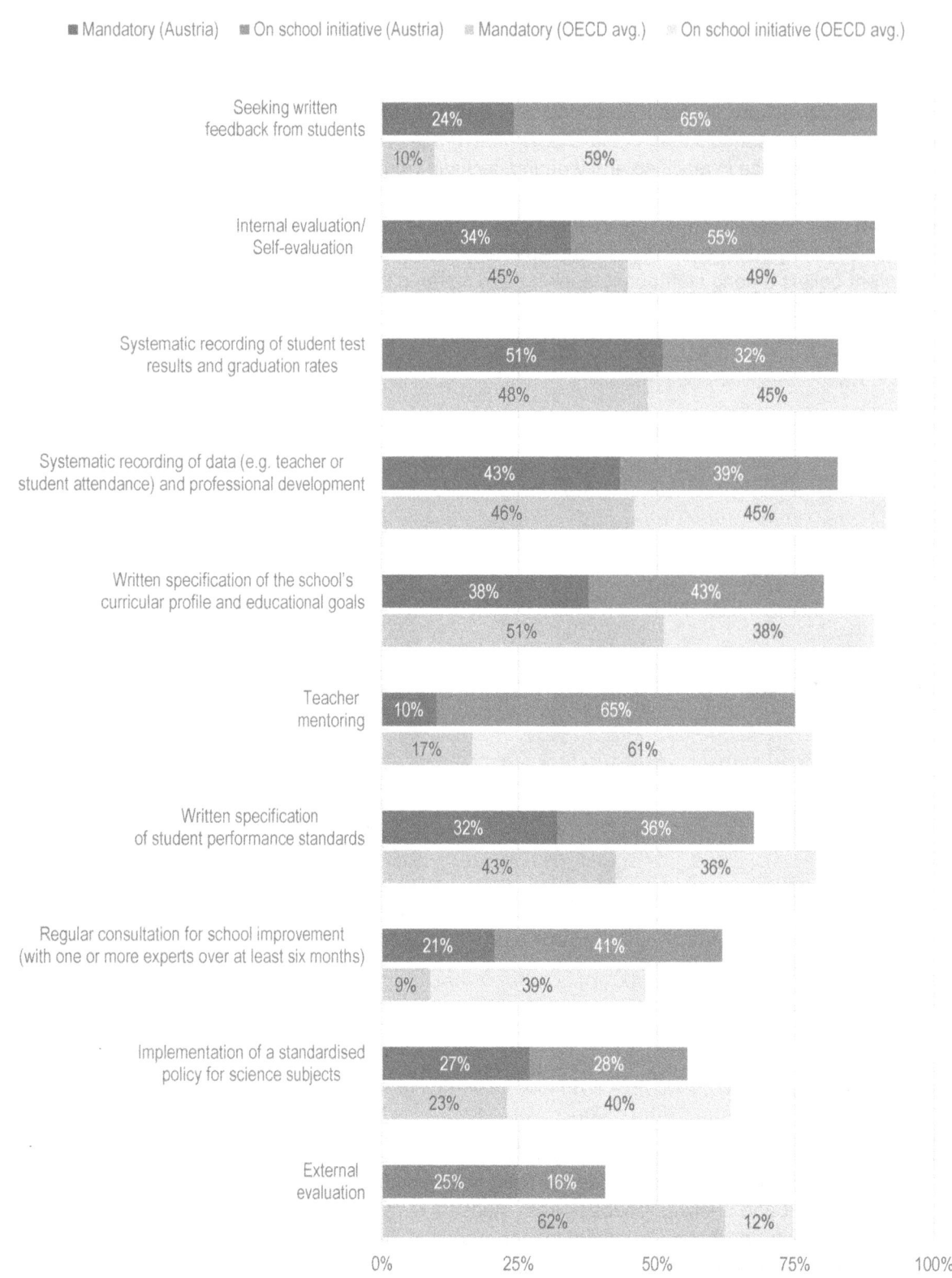

Source: Compiled from Table II.4.33 in OECD (2016[2]) PISA 2015 Results (Volume II): Policies and Practices for Successful Schools

Reports also show an increase in the use of student tests to monitor teaching practices between 2003 and 2012. Similar to their international counterparts, Austrian lower secondary teachers who report multiple methods of feedback on their teaching are more likely to find this has a positive impact on their teaching practices (OECD, 2020[5]).

A primary source of evidence in all schools is, of course, student assessments. Austrian school leader reports in 2015 indicate comparatively greater use of tests/assessment for summative assessment of individual students. There is widely reported use of tests/assessments for awarding certificates to students or deciding on their retention or promotion, greater than on average in the OECD. However, it is of note that teacher-developed tests are less frequently used than in the OECD on average, with more reliance on teacher judgemental ratings (OECD, 2016[2]). In light of the central role that teachers play in student assessment, it is striking that comparatively fewer Austrian lower secondary teachers reported that feedback on their practices had led to a positive change in using student assessments to improve student learning (32% in Austria; 50% in the OECD on average) (OECD, 2020[5]).

However, compared to on average in the OECD, there is less reported use of student assessment results for monitoring and comparing school performance. Austrian school leader reports in 2015 indicate that the use of standardised tests is far less prominent in Austrian schools, compared to average in the OECD (Table 4.1). However, in 2015 nearly two-thirds of students were in schools where the school leader reports that students achievement data are tracked over time by an administrative authority (OECD, 2016[2]).

Table 4.1. Uses of student test results in Austria compared to OECD average (PISA 2015)

Percentage of students in schools where the school principal reported the following uses of tests or assessments

	Standardised tests		Teacher-developed tests	
	Austria	OECD average	Austria	OECD average
Guide students' learning	37%	63%	95%	94%
Inform parents about their child's progress	32%	62%	83%	92%
Make decisions about students' retention or promotion	12%	31%	87%	71%
Award certificates to students	16%	40%	84%	55%
Adapt teaching to students' needs	27%	52%	71%	86%
Identify aspects of instruction or curriculum that could be improved	22%	59%	45%	73%
Group students for instructional purposes	7%	30%	25%	57%
Make judgements about teachers' effectiveness	15%	37%	25%	39%
Monitor the school's progress from year to year	28%	69%	44%	56%
Compare the school to district or national performance	21%	68%	9%	21%
Compare the school with other schools	18%	60%	6%	17%

Note: The results presented here are for those who answered 'Yes' and are not adjusted for non-response, which was less than 2% for all uses except adapting to student needs (3%), comparing with other schools (3%) and identifying aspects of instruction for improvement (2%).
Source: Compiled from Table II.4.24 in OECD (2016[2]) PISA 2015 Results (Volume II): Policies and Practices for Successful Schools

References

BMBWF (2019), *Steuerung des Schulsystems in Österreich: Weissbuch [Governance of the Education System in Austria: White Paper]*, Bundesministerium für Bildung, Wissenschaft und Forschung, Abt. III/3, http://www.bmbwf.gv.at. [4]

Nusche, D. et al. (2016), *OECD Reviews of School Resources: Austria 2016*, OECD Reviews of School Resources, OECD Publishing, Paris, https://dx.doi.org/10.1787/9789264256729-en. [6]

OECD (2020), *TALIS 2018 Results (Volume II): Teachers and School Leaders as Valued Professionals*, TALIS, OECD Publishing, Paris, https://dx.doi.org/10.1787/19cf08df-en. [5]

OECD (2018), *Education at a Glance 2018: OECD Indicators*, OECD Publishing, Paris, https://dx.doi.org/10.1787/eag-2018-en. [3]

OECD (2016), *PISA 2015 Results (Volume II): Policies and Practices for Successful Schools*, PISA, OECD Publishing, Paris, https://dx.doi.org/10.1787/9789264267510-en. [2]

OECD (2012), *Education at a Glance 2012: OECD Indicators*, OECD Publishing, Paris, https://dx.doi.org/10.1787/eag-2012-en. [1]

5 Promoting the use of evidence in Austria's education system

This section analyses the results of the online survey among key decision makers in the Austrian education system. The survey gauged the presence of efforts and opportunities that empirical research finds to promote decision makers' use of evidence. The section is structured around decision makers in policy (executives in the federal ministry and education directorates), quality assurance (school quality managers) and schools (school leaders).

The Federal Ministry for Education, Science and Research (*Bundesministerium für Bildung, Wissenschaft und Forschung*, BMBWF), with the support of a group of graduate students of the Vienna University of Economics and Business, carried out an online survey among key decision makers in the Austrian education system in November 2019. The survey is adapted for use in the Austrian context from the Knowledge Governance module of the OECD's policy toolkit for strategic education governance. The OECD, in cooperation with the BMBWF, developed questionnaire adaptations for four different target groups. Two first target groups for the survey were decision makers at the BMBWF itself and in the education directorate in each province. Education directorates are carrying out jointly the executive responsibilities of the provinces and the federal ministry in education. School quality managers (SQMs) were a third target group. They are part of the education directorate in each province. Each province is divided in one or more Education Regions. SQMs take the place of former school supervision and take a regional focus. SQMs are responsible for optimising and coordinating the education offer within a given Education Region. They support schools in their quality assurance based on a quality management system common to all school types and exert a supervisory function in relation to school leaders. A fourth target group were school leaders. Regarding this most numerous group, the 2017 Education Reform Act increased autonomy of schools to better cater to the local needs of students (BMBWF, 2019[1]).

The different adaptations for these groups comprised about 25 questions each. They were divided into the five areas that promote the capability, motivation, and opportunity to use evidence in decision making:

1. The skills to access and make sense of evidence.
2. Making relevant evidence conveniently available to decision makers.
3. Fostering the organisational processes and structures that encourage use of evidence.
4. Fostering the exchange among decision makers and their exchange with evidence producers, and
5. Promoting use of evidence as a principle of good decision-making, building a shared understanding on what constitutes fit-for-purpose evidence, as well as how and when evidence should be used.

The survey included further introductory questions that relate to current evidence use of the respective target group and closed with an open question for further suggestions and innovative examples. The questionnaires were sent out to 72 executives of the federal ministry, 27 executives from the education directorates, 163 school quality managers (SQM) and 5 745 Austrian school leaders. Overall, around half of all decision makers asked to participate completed the questionnaire (47%).

Using evidence in the federal ministry and education directorates

Half of executives of the BMBWF (35 of 72, 49%) and two-thirds of education directors (17 of 27, 63%) responded to their respective adaption of the questionnaire. The education directorates are a new administrative authority for the education sector in any one province, bringing together the previously dispersed administrative tasks of the federal Government and the given province (*Land*). The education directorates are responsible for the overall implementation of school legislation. This includes quality assurance through school supervision and school development in the form of school quality managers (SQM). The Federal Ministry of Education, Science and Research (BMBWF) is set to oversee external school evaluation/ inspection, which is to be distinct from tasks carried out by school quality managers (school supervision) (BMBWF, 2019[1]).

Decision makers in the federal ministry (BMBWF) overwhelmingly consider use of evidence to be not yet as extensive in the education system as it could be. Education directors are likewise keen to expand the use of evidence in the system. In terms of using evidence, virtually all decision makers in the federal ministry and education directorates rely frequently or regularly on evidence in their work. They use varied resources to access relevant evidence. This includes dedicated departments within the federal ministry and education directorate, respectively. Education directorates work closely with the federal ministry directly to access relevant evidence. Decision makers carry out their own research, as well as make use of out-contracted research and external experts. Resources also include national institutes (such as the Federal Institute for Educational Research, Innovation and Development BIFIE)[1] and international organisations (such as OECD, EU, and Non-Governmental Organisations). Decision makers also reach out to universities and, to a lesser extent, university colleges of teacher education to inform their decisions.

Building the skills for effective evidence use at the BMBWF and education directorates

Developing the skills to make sense of evidence are crucial to consider evidence systematically in daily decision making. Decision makers in the federal ministry rely on exchange with colleagues and report (external) professional development to help them acquire skills to use evidence effectively. To develop their skills to better instruct their staff in the use of evidence, decision makers in education directorates and the federal ministry report (external) professional development as the most widely available opportunity.

Around a third of decision makers who completed the survey in federal ministry and education directorates is aware of professional development opportunities tailored to their role as supervisors to build these skills. Another third is not aware of any opportunities to acquire skills to better make use of evidence or supervise the use of evidence. This may suggest that respective opportunities are not systematically available for all decision makers or that their availability is not systematically communicated. Regarding efforts to build the skills to access and make sense of evidence, one senior decision maker at the federal ministry highlights:

> *"The department is developing a training programme on data literacy. In this area, there is a need for many more offers for in-house staff and for the education directorates, especially for SQM [school quality managers]".*

Organisational resources are crucial to help senior decision makers guide and instruct their staff's use of evidence and encourage staff to acquire skills relevant to make better use of evidence in decision making. This includes access and use of competency frameworks, instructions/guidance on how to carry out staff reviews to foster evidence use, and staff development measures to encourage staff to develop their skills to use evidence. Decision makers in the federal ministry appear to be not systematically aware of or able to draw on resources to help guide their staff in the use of evidence. Only a quarter of decision makers in the federal ministry is aware of any one measure to support them in this task. More than 40% of decision makers are not aware of any resources to guide their staff in the use of evidence.

Making evidence available

Untargeted communication of evidence – or access to evidence, for instance through databases – can make it difficult for the audience of decision makers to identify the most relevant elements for their practice. Beyond targeting groups of decision makers, tailoring evidence to decision makers' specific preferences and work habits can further increase convenience and thus improve the uptake.

The federal ministry does not systematically target evidence to different groups. While half of senior decision makers who completed the questionnaire reported that the federal ministry mostly targets different groups, a third of respondents reports that the ministry does little to target its evidence to specific groups. Where the BMBWF tailors evidence to the needs and habits of its audience, it largely focuses on topics/content, communication channels and, to a lesser extent, different levels of experience with using evidence.

In contrast, adapting evidence to user needs is high on the agenda for education directorates, with over two-thirds of decision makers reporting to this effect. Well over half of decision makers in education directorates who completed the survey report to tailor evidence to target groups such as school quality managers, school leaders, teachers or the general public. Education directorates report to tailor evidence largely along different levels of experience in using evidence and interest in different topics among target groups.

Consulting the audience in preparing evidence can help improve its relevance, as well as the motivation and ease of using evidence. This may include consultation over relevant topics and preferred communication channels and type of preparation (such as databases, newsletters, information material, or advisory services). Equally, involving stakeholders in the preparation of evidence can include soliciting content (such as writing articles for a publication). Stakeholders may also be included in evaluation efforts. Overall, education directorates involve others to a greater extent in their preparation of evidence. However, the BMBWF puts greater emphasis on involving teachers in evaluation efforts related to preparing its evidence (Figure 5.1).

Figure 5.1. Involving stakeholders in making evidence available in BMBWF/ education directorates

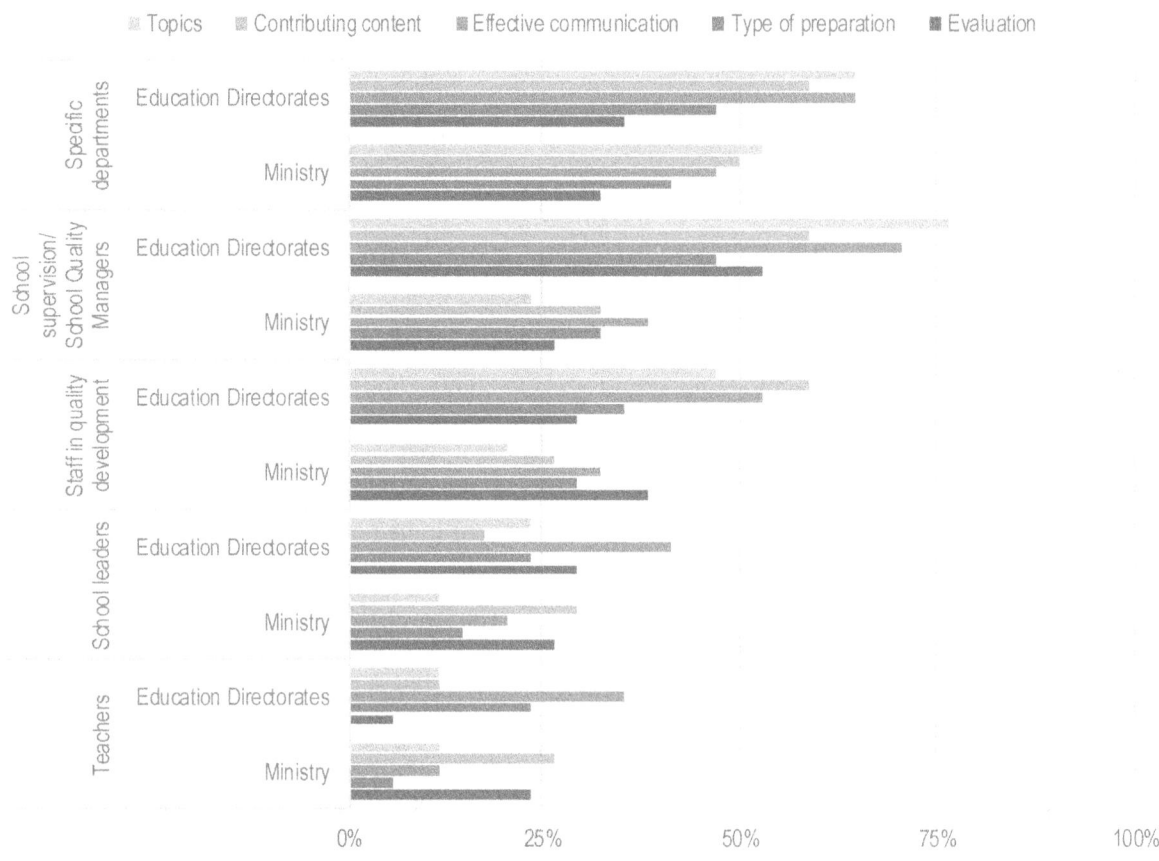

Note: Follow-up question drawing on positive responses to question "The [ministry] [education directorate] involves the users of evidence in the preparation of evidence". Responses to the question "With regard to which aspects does the [ministry] [education directorate] involve the listed user groups?" N=**22** (ministry), N=**14** (education directorates).

Organisational processes

Organisational processes are relevant to efforts to promote the use of evidence mainly by encouraging its use. This includes promoting transparency of decision-making processes (for instance, through publishing decision-making procedures or direct exchange with stakeholders to make decisions plain) and involving different perspectives and stakeholders in decision making. Compared to the BMBWF, education directorates are found to engage more frequently in measures to create transparency around decision processes and involving internal and external stakeholders.

Efforts to clarify decisions and decision-making processes focus on internal exchange

The BMBWF and the education directorates work to make decisions plain and decision-making processes transparent mainly through internal exchange. Within the federal ministry, three-quarters of decision makers who completed the survey reported so. Virtually all education directors engage in exchange within their directorate to clarify decisions. Engaging with other stakeholders to this effect is likewise relatively widespread in the federal ministry and the education directorates, with close to two-thirds of decision makers engaging with (external) stakeholders. Decision makers in the BMBWF and education directorates also mention (publicly) available documents to clarify decision making. Making use of published documents to create transparency is more widespread in education directorates (60% vs. 35%).

Involving different perspectives in decision making can encourage greater use of evidence; by opening the decision-making process to stakeholders or by being encouraged to consider their perspectives in greater detail. Overall in the federal ministry and education directorates, diverse perspectives are more frequently involved in substantive decision-making areas of preparing, implementing and evaluating measures. In comparison with each other, education directorates put greater emphasis on internal processes of staff and organisational development than the ministry. However, the ministry involves different perspectives in evaluation more frequently than education directorates (Figure 5.2).

Figure 5.2. Involving diverse perspectives in decision making in BMBWF/ education directorates

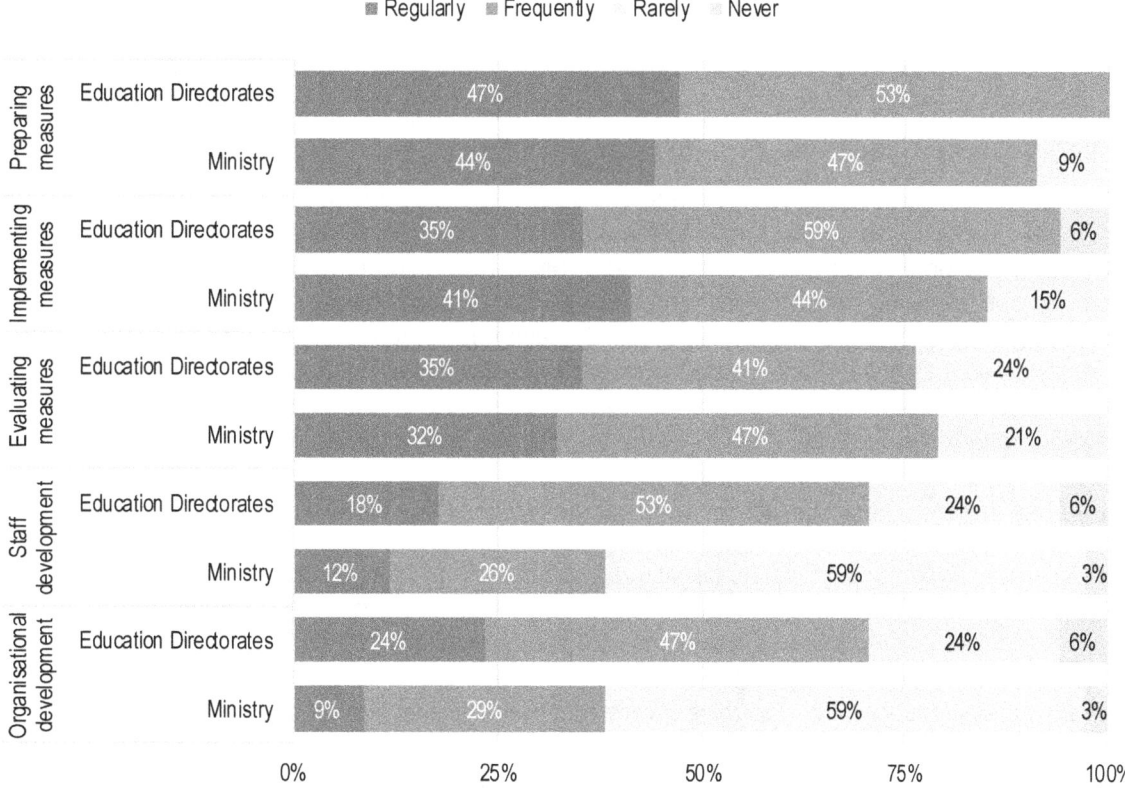

Note: N=34 (ministry), N=17 (education directorates). Answer to question "In which processes of the [ministry] [education directorate] are different perspectives (internal/external) taken into account or explicitly included in decision making?".

Awareness of knowledge management systems could be more systematic

Knowledge management systems help contextualise evidence and link knowledge across and within organisations for access by decision makers where needed. This can include general data management, a collection of organisational procedures, or other knowledge relevant to the functioning of the organisation and the decision-making processes at hand. Today, knowledge management systems are predominantly computer-based but likewise include printed material.

The focus of knowledge management is on systems to exchange and contextualise information within the ministry and education directorates. Online project tools, cloud services and an office suite are specifically identified as knowledge management systems. To make the best use of knowledge management systems, respective systems should be available to all decision makers and all decision makers should be aware of available systems. Decision makers across ministry and education directorates appear not systematically aware of available knowledge management systems. While a quarter of decision makers identified knowledge management available to them across organisations, a third of decision makers who completed the survey were not aware of any knowledge management system at their disposal, suggesting that decision makers do not have a common understanding of knowledge management systems.

Exchanging with colleagues to promote evidence use in decision making

Half of decision makers in the federal ministry and the education directorates who completed the survey report regular opportunities to exchange informally with colleagues regarding experiences and methods around using evidence. However, 14 of the 34 (40%) decision makers in the ministry who completed the survey, report not to have opportunities to exchange with colleagues informally or in organisationally established exchanges about using evidence in their work. Education directors report opportunities more frequently (75%) and fewer decision makers report to be without opportunities to exchange with colleagues about their experiences and methods to use evidence for their work (17%).

Exchanges with colleagues cover a wide range of topics. Topics include encouraging greater consideration of evidence, developing common standards for considering evidence in decision making, and improving quality or preparation of evidence. Of those in the ministry who report exchanges with colleagues around methods and experience around using evidence, 45% emphasise that these exchanges focus on strengthening the use of evidence in decision making and improving the preparation of evidence. Similar to the ministry, education directors emphasise in exchanges with colleagues how to encourage the use of evidence. Half of education directors who reported opportunities to exchange with colleague emphasise the development of common standards for using evidence as topic of these discussions.

Developing common standards for using evidence

Efforts to raise awareness of evidence use as a principle of good decision making are relatively widespread. This can include distributing information material on the merits and importance of considering evidence in decision making as well as events and initiatives to this effect. It may also include advisory services that include elements to raise awareness, or dedicated advisory for school quality managers (SQM) and school leaders on how to raise awareness among those with which they work. For SQMs this would include raising awareness for the merits of using evidence among schools; for school leaders this pertains to raising respective awareness among their teaching staff. Raising awareness is high on the agenda. As one education director highlights,

> *Evidence-based work is important, but in the future it needs an even stronger focus and awareness to see this as a basis for everyday work.*

Distribution of information material is the most popular means to raise awareness followed by events and initiatives. Overall, education directorates engage more systemically in efforts to raise awareness, in particular in terms of providing advice and organising events for SQMs and school leaders to raise awareness and help them in turn to raise awareness (Figure 5.3).

Figure 5.3. Efforts by BMBWF/ education directorates raising awareness for using evidence

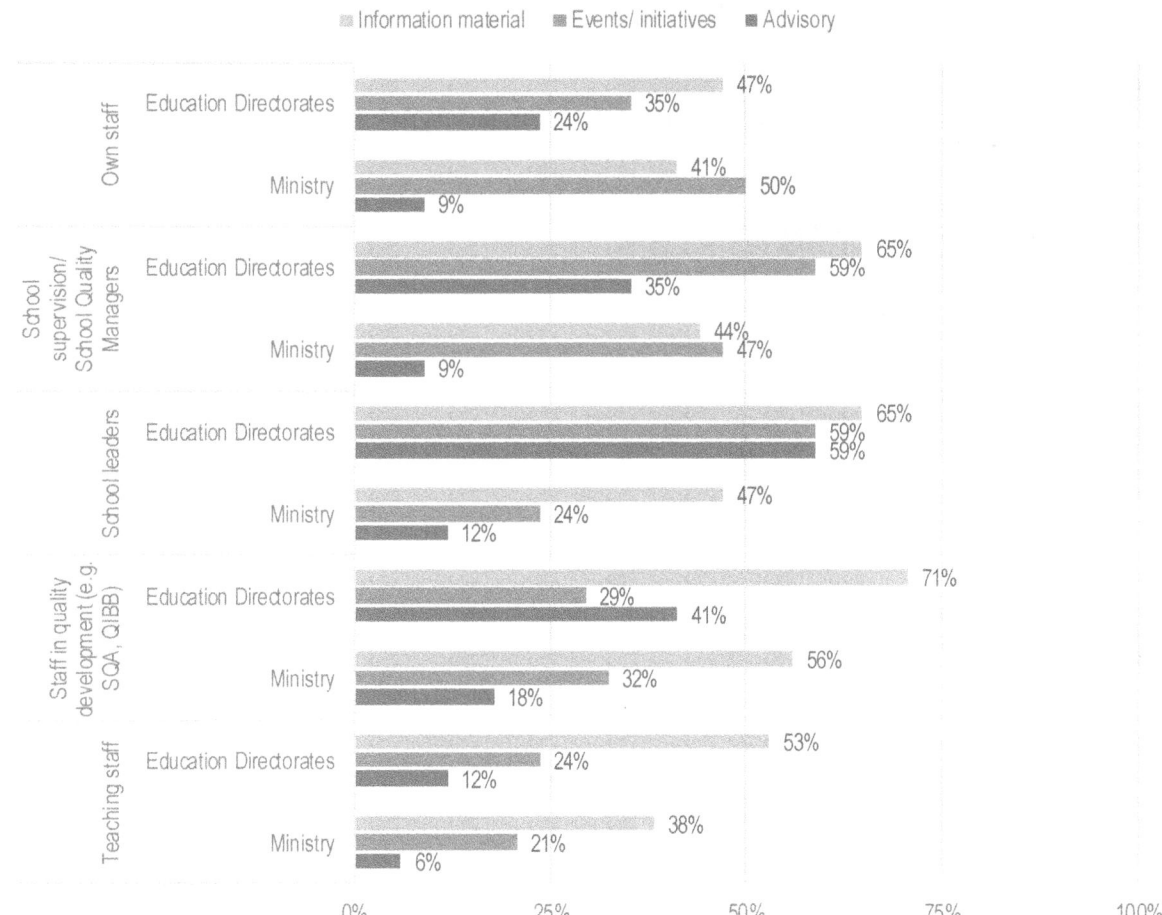

Note: Follow-up question drawing on positive responses to question "In your opinion, does the ministry take measures to raise awareness of the use of evidence as a basis for decision making?". Answers to question "Which awareness-raising measures are implemented for which target groups?" Multiple answers possible. N=**21** (ministry), N=**14** (education directorates).

Emergent efforts to develop a common understanding how evidence should be used in specific decision-making areas

Efforts to create a common understanding how evidence should be used in concrete decision-making areas and respective challenges are emergent. About half of decision makers in the ministry who completed the survey are not aware of any efforts to this effect or feel they cannot judge whether such efforts exist. Individual decision makers already engage in respective efforts in various decision-making areas. This includes decisions in preparing, implementing and evaluating measures, as well as staff development and governance decisions. Within these areas, efforts to develop common standards how to use evidence focus on governance decisions as one of the central responsibilities of the ministry and education directorates (Figure 5.4).

Figure 5.4. BMBWF/ education directorates developing common understanding of using evidence

Efforts in specific areas of decision making to develop common understanding of how evidence should be used

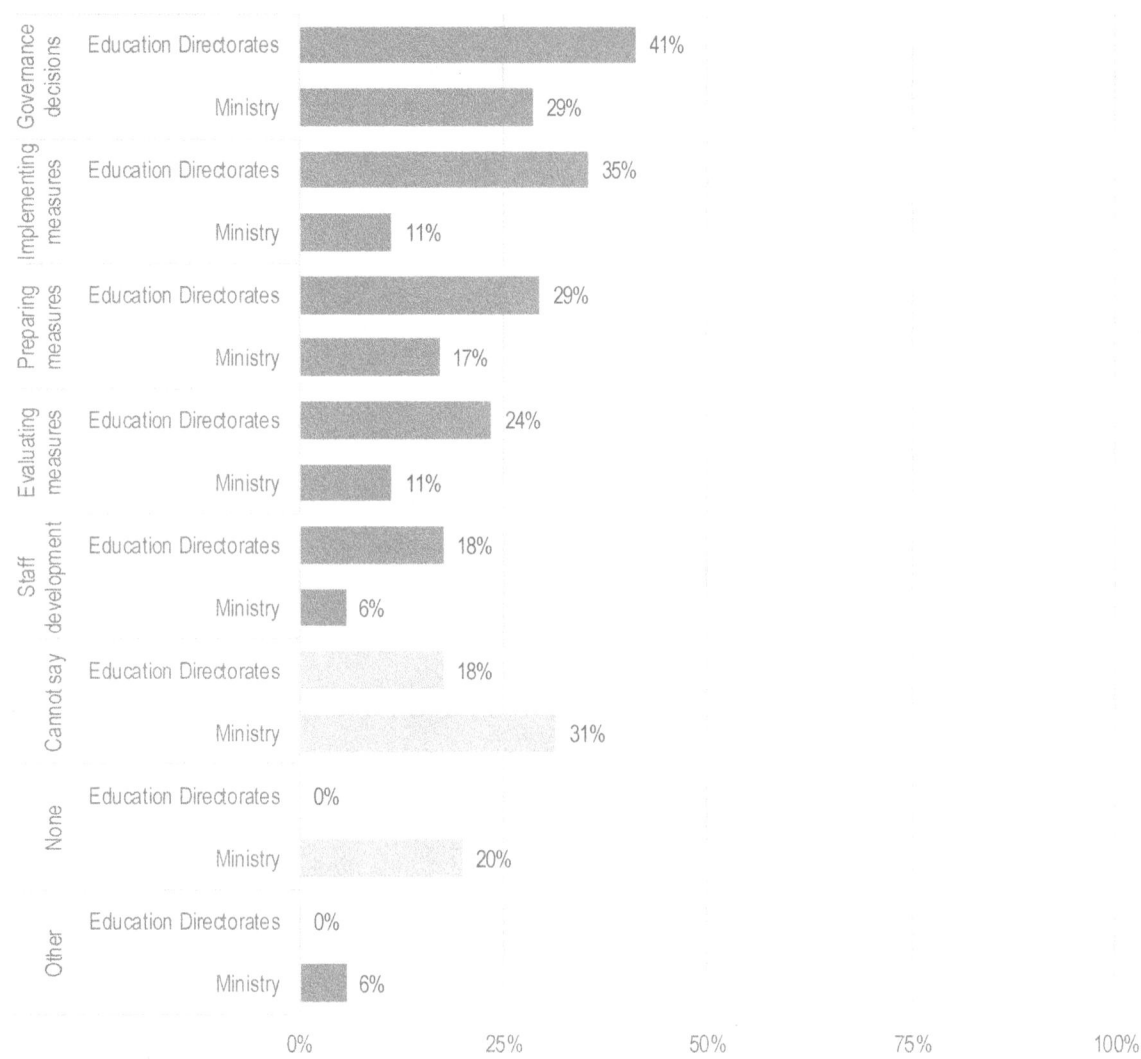

Note: N=34 (BMBWF), N=17 (education directorates). Answer to question "Are there efforts within the [ministry] [education directorates] to develop a common understanding of how evidence should be used in concrete decision-making situations?" Multiple answers possible.

School quality managers – evidence use at the intersection of school and regional development

Almost two-thirds (64%, 104 of 163) of school quality managers completed the survey across 31 education regions. Administrative arrangements are diverse regarding number of Education Regions in each province and the number of school quality managers overseeing education regions in any one province (Table 5.1). More than half (57%) of the responding SQMs work as school supervisors between two and ten years. More than 30% have even been working in this position for more than ten years. 12% of SQMs worked less than two years in their current position.

Table 5.1. Number of education regions, school quality managers and response rate by province

Province	Number of schools	Education regions	Number of school quality managers (SQM)	Responses	Response rate
Burgenland	275	1	9	6	67%
Carinthia	389	2	13	6	46%
Lower Austria	1232	6	32	14	44%
Upper Austria	1021	6	30	27	90%
Salzburg	382	2	11	5	45%
Styria	844	7	23	10	43%
Tyrol	631	3	13	11	85%
Vorarlberg	291	2	8	8	100%
Vienna	680	2	24	17	71%
Overall	**5745**	**31**	**164**	**104**	**64%**

Sources: Own data; BMBWF (2019[1]) *Steuerung des Schulsystems in Österreich: Weissbuch [Governance of the Education System in Austria: White Paper]*, Bundesministerium für Bildung, Wissenschaft und Forschung, Abt. III/3, http://www.bmbwf.gv.at.

Developing skills to use evidence for quality assurance and supporting schools

The skills to access and make sense of evidence are crucial to consider evidence systematically in daily decision making. Overall, opportunities to build skills to access and make sense of evidence are widely available to school quality managers. Opportunities focus on diverse training offers and exchange with colleagues over mentoring/coaching and e-learning/learning platforms. School quality managers rely on previous studies, ongoing studies as well as individual coursework at universities to ensure they have the requisite skills to access and make sense of evidence for their daily work. They engage with regional university colleges of teacher education and individual university staff to build their skills.

What school quality managers frequently report lacking are opportunities to build skills to guide and instruct evidence use of their staff and of the schools with which they work. SQMs with the requisite skills to guide and instruct the use of evidence can motivate their staff as well as schools to make better use of evidence and to acquire relevant skills. Overall, close to a third of school quality managers report that there are no opportunities to build these skills specifically. On the upper end, this is the case for 10 out of the 17 school quality managers in Vienna. Reflecting this scarcity, individual school quality managers specifically pointed out they rely on their own initiative to build these skills, for example through engaging in self-study.

Varied resources to guide and instruct the use of evidence – with regional differences

Important for effective instruction and supervision of evidence use is that school quality managers can rely on organisational resources to support them in this task. This includes education and training requirements for staff, instructions for conducting reviews, and the possibility to initiate related development measures (Langer, Tripney and Gough, 2016[2]; Gray et al., 2012[3]). School quality managers report varied such resources available, though with substantial regional differences in which resources are available and in the degree to which these are systematically available to SQMs. School quality managers centrally guide and instruct school leaders in the use of evidence. SQM further oversee their staff's use of evidence within their respective responsibilities. The SQM team in an education region includes diversity managers as well as administrative staff.

About half of all school quality managers report education and training requirements that include competencies related to evidence use to support them in instructing use of evidence. SQMs report to a similar degree that they have access to guidelines on how to conduct staff reviews with the aim to foster the use of evidence. About a third of school quality managers report that they have the possibility to initiate staff development measures related to use of evidence.

Competency development requirements appear systematically available and known to SQMs in Burgenland and Styria with over 80% of SQMs reporting them as available. Guidelines to make use of staff appraisal to promote use of evidence are systematically available to SQMs in Styria and Vorarlberg. Despite at a lower degree, still over half of all SQMs in Salzburg and Tyrol report both competency development requirements guidelines for staff appraisal as resources available to them. In the remaining provinces, resources appear unsystematically available, with only 50% or fewer SQMs reporting any one instrument available to them. In particular, in Vienna and Upper Austria, over a third of SQMs report that no resources are available to support them in instructing and guiding their staff's use of evidence.

As part of their school supervision function, school quality managers have the task of guiding and instructing schools in the use of evidence. The school-internal evaluation is a legal obligation of the school which includes the use of the data for school development. In the context of performance measurements, it is the task of school leaders to define the development areas. The use of evidence, the school development measures derived from it and their results are important topics in the performance review and objective-setting discussions (BZG) between SQM and school leaders.[2]

To help school quality managers guide and instruct the use of evidence by the schools with which they work, school quality managers highlight the SAND tool (*Schulentwicklung durch Analyse und Nutzung von Daten*; School development through analysis and use of data). The tool and respective trainings present a resource to guide and instruct use of evidence. SQMs also report their engagement with *Schulentwicklungsberater/-innen* (school development advisors) and *Rückmeldemoderatoren/-innen* (feedback moderators) as an important resource helping them guide and instruct schools in their use of evidence for quality development. Moreover, school quality managers note the *Bilanz- und Zielvereinbarungsgespräch* (BZG, performance review and objective-setting discussion) as an instrument to support them in guiding and instructing schools in the use of evidence.

Making evidence available for decisions at the intersection of schools and regional level

School quality managers (SQM) work at the intersection of supporting schools and regional development. On the one hand, this requires work with evidence close to schools to support their quality development. This includes support of schools' and their staff's professional development as well as organisational development. On the other, school quality managers require evidence to optimise the education and support measures offered to students in the region, and allocate resource across their region.

> *School quality managers largely consider evidence as well prepared for their work but wish for more involvement to improve preparation and provision of evidence*

Making evidence available pertains to supporting SQMs through providing relevant and adequately prepared evidence for their work at this intersection. This should entail BMBWF, BIFIE and other institutions working together with SQMs to identify which evidence is most relevant and in which form it is most user-friendly. On the other hand, this means supporting and encouraging SQMs to engage on their own initiative in bringing together and preparing evidence for their work.

SQMs regard the availability and user-friendliness of evidence with which they are provided largely positive. Overall, around 60% of SQMs largely or fully agree that evidence is well prepared for their work. Around a third of SQMs praise the evidence prepared by research institutions, such as BIFIE and university colleges of teacher education as highly user-friendly. Around half of SQMs perceive the evidence provided BMBWF and education directorates as largely user-friendly.

Given requisite capabilities, local decision makers are best placed to identify which evidence in which form can help them best to develop actionable knowledge for decision-making challenges at hand in the specific local context (Langer, Tripney and Gough, 2016[2]; Burns, Köster and Fuster, 2016[4]; Shewbridge and Köster, 2019[5]). Moreover, school quality managers face a change in their responsibilities from the 2017 governance reform. Effective and efficient work processes and habits take time to emerge. Needs regarding evidence are not fully known from the beginning and emerge over time in the process of day-to-day decision making.

Figure 5.5. Main evidence providers and sources of evidence used by school quality managers

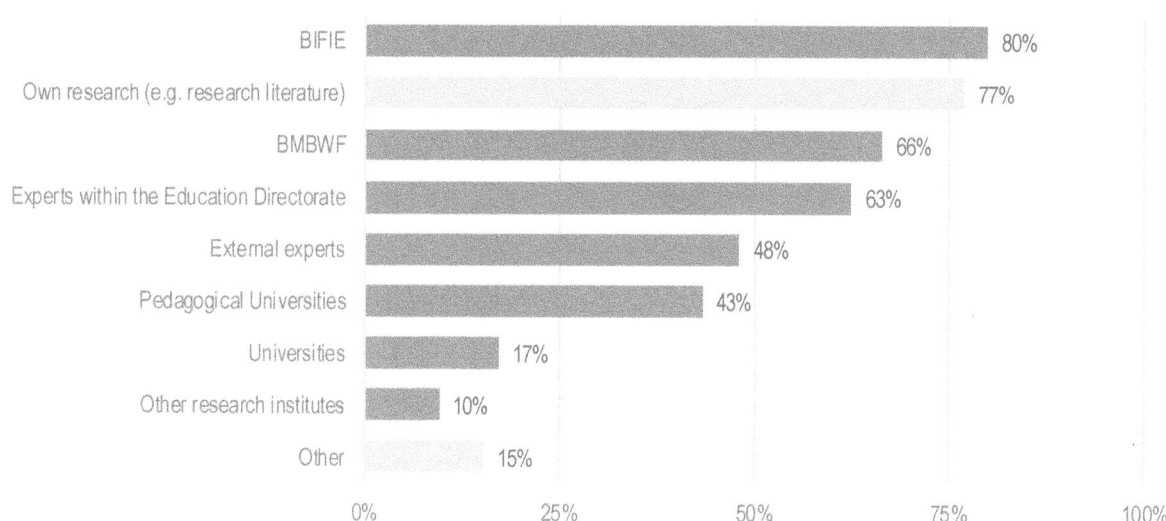

Note: N=104. Share of answers to question "As School Quality Manager, how do you access the evidence relevant to you?". Multiple answers possible. Categories pertaining to evidence on SQMs initiative in light blue. 'Other' includes school administrative data, direct engagement with schools and school leaders, interviews with school graduates, parents, students, teachers and others.

School quality managers would like to be involved to a greater extend in the provision and preparation of evidence. Only 30% of SQMs largely or fully agree to feeling adequately involved in providing and preparing evidence. However, regional differences are pronounced. In Carinthia and Vorarlberg, no SQM feels more than marginally involved[3]. On the other end, in Salzburg and Burgenland, over six out of ten SQM largely or fully agree to being sufficiently involved. In particular, SQMs wish for more involvement in deciding on relevant topics as well adequate communication channels. SQMs in Upper Austria show the greatest demand for more involvement over all. Here, half of all SQM wish for more involvement in defining topics, improving communication channels, effective formats, as well as the evaluation of evidence provision.

Beyond evidence made available to them, SQMs engage with evidence on their own initiative. More than 75% of SQMs engage with research to create or revise their knowledge, such as through working with research literature. Over 15% of SQMs report to engage in bringing together evidence themselves. This includes evidence from schools such as school administrative data and direct engagement with schools and school leaders as well as interviews with school graduates, parents, students, and teachers (Figure 5.5).

At the intersection between school support and regional development, school quality managers engage in their own preparation evidence for their work. Preparing evidence to support schools in their quality development is more widespread. Three-quarters of SQMs work up evidence themselves to support schools' development and professionalising schools and their staff. Around 40% engage in working up evidence related to regional development (Figure 5.6).

Figure 5.6. Tasks for which school quality managers prepare evidence themselves

Note: N=104. Share of answers to question "Do you prepare evidence yourself?". Multiple answers possible. Categories pertaining to evidence to support schools' development in light blue. 'Other' includes preparing performance review and objective-setting discussions (*Bilanz- und Zielvereinbarungsgespräche*, BZG), analysing educational opportunities, resource planning, evaluating development plans.

Organisational processes to foster the use of evidence in school quality assurance

Organisational processes within the education directorates and the Education Regions can encourage the use of evidence in decision making in school quality assurance. This pertains to clarifying decisions and how these were reached, inviting additional perspectives into decision making as well as being able to rely on knowledge management systems that help contextualise evidence to develop actionable knowledge.

> *School quality managers clarify how decisions were reached to stakeholders and – with regional differences – involve diverse perspectives in decision making*

Around 70% of school quality managers report at least one measure to make decisions-making processes plain and make clear how decisions were reached. Most widespread are exchange formats within the Education Region. Over half of school quality managers are involved in respective exchanges. This can include exchanges with schools and stakeholders, as well as colleagues within the Education Region. Similar exchange processes with other colleagues within the education directorate are less common. Respective processes are reported by about one-third of school quality managers. Only about 10% of school quality managers report efforts to make decisions plain through (publicly) available documentation of the process behind decisions.

Overall, school quality managers involve or explicitly consider perspectives of different internal or external stakeholders mainly in substantive areas of decision-making (preparing, implementing and evaluating activities). Involvement is slightly lower in internal processes, in particular when concerning staff development. School quality managers' use of evidence across areas of decision-making follows a similar pattern (Figure 5.7).

Figure 5.7. SQMs' involving of diverse perspectives in decision making and use of evidence

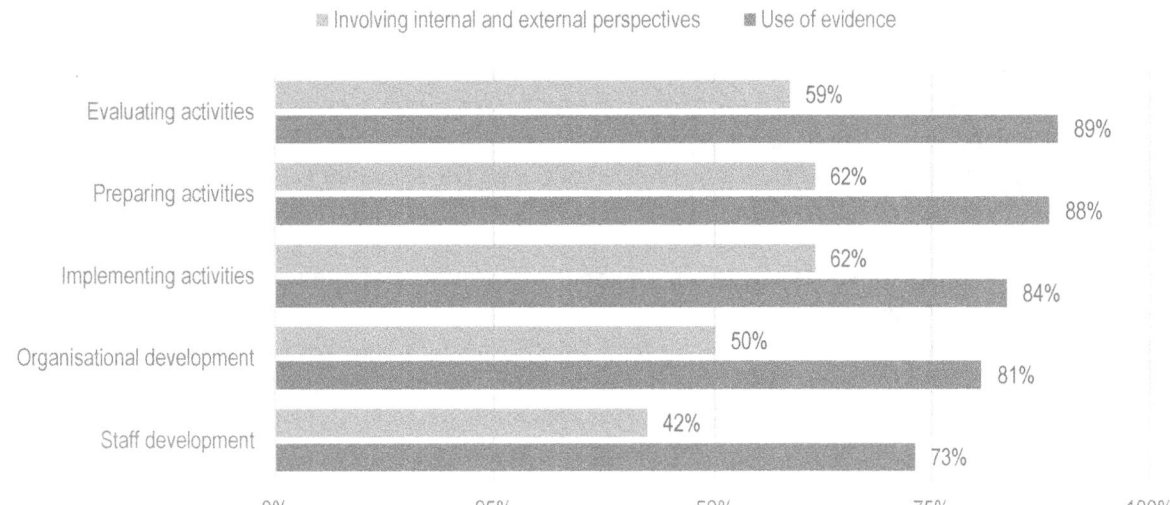

Note: N=104. Share of answers to questions "In which processes in the Education Region are different perspectives (internal/external) taken into account or involved in decision-making?" and "As School Quality Manager, how often do you use evidence in the following areas?" (Cumulated answers Regularly/Frequently). Multiple answers possible.

In some provinces, school quality managers prioritise individual areas of decision making in which they involve or explicitly consider diverse perspectives. Contrary to the average, SQMs in Burgenland emphasise organisational development and staff development. Here, all six school quality managers who answered the survey, report to involve diverse perspectives frequently or regularly in respective decisions. In Vorarlberg and Vienna, SQMs emphasise the preparation of measures. In either province, over 80% of SQMs report to involve or explicitly consider diverse perspectives frequently or regularly in respective decision-making, compared to around 50% across the remaining decision-making areas.

Limited awareness of knowledge management systems among school quality managers

Knowledge management systems help contextualise evidence and link knowledge across and within organisations for access by decision makers where needed. This can include general data management, a collection of organisational procedures, or other knowledge relevant to the functioning of the organisation and the decision-making processes at hand. Today, knowledge management systems are predominantly computer-based but likewise include printed material. To make best use of knowledge management systems, respective systems should be available to all decision makers and all decision makers should be aware of available systems.

Among the 104 school quality managers who filled out the survey, about 70% report to have access to some form of knowledge management. This includes knowledge management systems to support SQMs in exchanging knowledge across the directorate and its (potentially) multiple Education Regions; systems to share knowledge within one Education Region; and systems allowing to link and exchange knowledge across different organisations. Awareness of available knowledge management systems varies greatly across provinces. In Salzburg, Tyrol and Styria virtually all school quality managers report at least one available knowledge management system. In Carinthia, Upper and Lower Austria, and Vienna, only around 60% of SQMs report access to at least one knowledge management system. Within provinces, knowledge of available knowledge management systems appears unsystematic. Overall, only 30%-50% of SQMs report any one individual type of knowledge management system, indicating that there may be no common understating of knowledge management systems.

Exchange with evidence providers

Variation in how systematically school quality managers exchange with evidence providers

On average, school quality managers in Salzburg, Styria and Vienna interact similarly frequently with evidence producers as in Burgenland. However, interaction is carried out less systematically, with some school quality managers reporting no engagement of quality management with evidence providers. In Burgenland, SQMs report systematically to interact about once per semester with evidence providers. In the remaining provinces, exchange between school quality managers and evidence providers appears relatively unsystematic. Here, some SQMs report to engage with evidence providers once a year or once per semester; in some cases, SQMs interact with evidence providers up to once a month as well as based on immediate needs. However, across provinces, between 25% and 60% of SQMs report no interaction with evidence providers. In eight provinces, the purpose of exchange between and SQMs and evidence providers systematically aims at improving the quality and preparation of the provided evidence. SQMs in Vorarlberg report a more ad-hoc and needs-based approach to exchange. Consistent with this approach, SQMs in Vorarlberg report the aim of improving the quality to a lesser extent.

Supporting the exchange between evidence providers and SQMs organisationally is important to promote the opportunity for exchange beyond individually initiated exchange. Overall, the exchange of SQMs with evidence providers appears not systematically supported. Organisational support in four out of the nine provinces is fragmented with some SQM reporting high and others reporting low levels of organisational support for their exchange with evidence providers. However, SQMs in a number of provinces report organisational support more systematically. This includes Burgenland, Tyrol, and Vienna, and, with lower frequency, Upper Austria and Vorarlberg.

Fostering the use evidence through collegial exchange

Exchange with colleagues can promote use of evidence through various channels. This includes encouraging use of evidence in decision-making through building awareness of its importance and fostering the motivation and capability to use evidence. Exchange among colleagues offers the opportunity to develop a common understanding for using evidence in decision-making. It further can be used to collaboratively identify and articulate issues with quality and preparation of evidence available to decision makers to improve communication and quality of evidence.

Over 80% of school quality managers engage in exchanges with colleagues working on school quality management to discuss experiences and methods related to using evidence. This includes encouraging the use of evidence, and exchanging insights about how preparation and quality of evidence could be improved. It also includes developing standards of how evidence should be used in decision-making (Figure 5.8). School quality managers set different emphases in their exchanges related to sharing experiences and methods of using evidence. SQMs in Tyrol and Lower Austria appear to emphasise improving preparation. In Burgenland and Upper Austria, exchanges focus on encouraging use of evidence. Exchanges among colleagues predominantly occur both in work meetings and in (regular) exchanges with colleagues that are more informal.

On average, only one in four school quality managers report as a topic of discussion in exchanges with colleagues the development of common standards regarding how evidence should be used in decision making (Figure 5.8). Contrary to the average, collegial exchanges among SQMs in Salzburg (80%) and Styria (50%) focus on developing common standards on how to use evidence as well as improving the quality of evidence.

Figure 5.8. The aims of collegial exchange among school quality managers

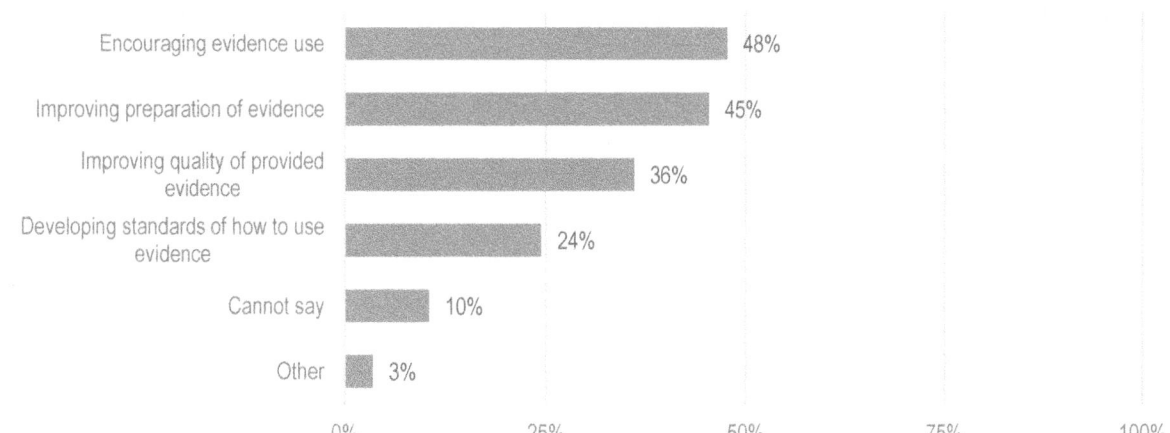

Note: Follow-up question drawing on positive responses to question "Are there opportunities to exchange with colleagues specifically regarding experiences and methods of using evidence?" Responses to question "Which aims do collegial exchanges pursue?". Multiple answers possible. N=**86**. Category aimed at developing common understanding of evidence (standards of how to use evidence) in light blue. 'Other' includes developing school and class teaching, and training/instruction in using SAND tool.

Similarly, efforts by school quality managers (SQM) to build a common understanding of how evidence should be used are relatively few. Across the various areas of decision making, around one-third of SQMs report respective efforts in substantive decision-making processes. The area of staff development, as an internal decision-making process, is reported slightly lower with about one in four school quality managers reporting respective efforts (Figure 5.9).

Figure 5.9. SQM's efforts in the education region to develop standards of how to use evidence

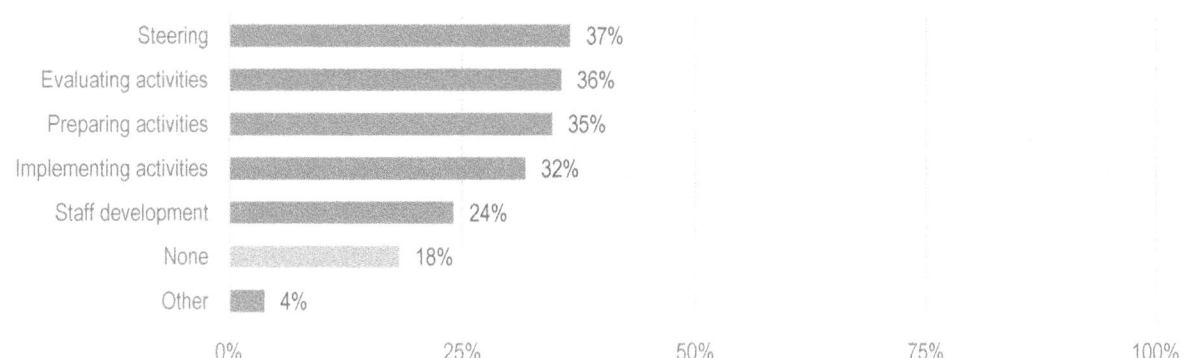

Note: N=104. Answers to question "Are there (initial) efforts in the education region to develop a common understanding of how evidence should be used in concrete decision-making situations?" Multiple answers possible.

Raising awareness of the merit and importance of using evidence in decision-making

More than 90% of school quality managers (97 out of 104) engage in efforts to build awareness for using evidence as a principle of good decision-making. SQMs engage school leaders, school staff responsible for quality assurance, as well as teachers in varied measures to build awareness for evidence. This includes work meetings, dedicated events and initiatives, offering advice on how to build awareness, and distributing information material. SQMs work primarily with school leaders, which is reflected in a clear focus of SQM to engage with school leaders to build awareness, in particular through work meetings. In addition, about six in ten school quality managers report to engage teaching staff in efforts to build awareness. This engagement of teachers focuses on distribution of information material. However, efforts of a quarter of SQMs include (also) events and initiatives aimed to build awareness (Figure 5.10).

Figure 5.10. Fostering awareness of using evidence as basis of good decision-making in schools

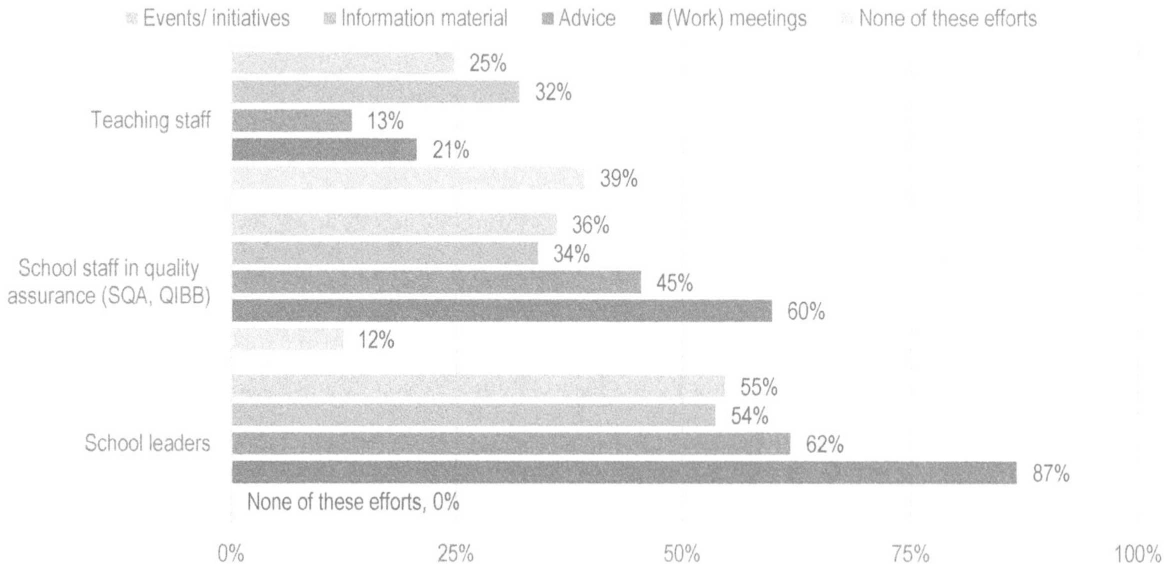

Teaching staff:
- Events/ initiatives: 25%
- Information material: 32%
- Advice: 13%
- (Work) meetings: 21%
- None of these efforts: 39%

School staff in quality assurance (SQA, QIBB):
- Events/ initiatives: 36%
- Information material: 34%
- Advice: 45%
- (Work) meetings: 60%
- None of these efforts: 12%

School leaders:
- Events/ initiatives: 55%
- Information material: 54%
- Advice: 62%
- (Work) meetings: 87%
- None of these efforts: 0%

Note: Follow-up question drawing on positive responses to question "As school quality manager, do you take measures to create awareness for the use of evidence as a basis for decisions?" Responses to question "Which measures do you initiate to develop awareness for evidence as basis for decision-making? For which groups do you initiate measures?" Multiple answers possible. N=**97**.

The use of evidence in schools

Overall, 46% of school leaders (2 651 of 5 745) completed the questionnaire. Some differences between school types are noticeable. Highest response rates are observed in lower secondary schools (NMS) and upper secondary general education schools (AHS). In terms of response rates, special-needs schools (ASO), lower and upper secondary vocational schools (BMHS) and part-time vocational schools of the dual system (BS) bring up the rear (Table 5.2). School size as reported by school leaders varies greatly across school types (Figure 5.11).

Table 5.2. School leader response rates by school type

School type	Number of schools	Share of all schools	Responses	Response rate
VS	2985	52%	1362	46%
NMS	1101	19%	597	54%
PTS	174	3%	78	45%
AHS	356	6%	189	53%
BMHS	590	10%	226	38%
BS	147	3%	58	39%
ASO	241	4%	90	37%
Other schools	151	3%	51	34%
Overall	**5745**	**100%**	**2651**	**46%**

Note: School type abbreviations refer to primary schools (*Volksschule*, VS), lower secondary schools (*Neue Mittelschule*, NMS), upper secondary general education schools (*Allgemein bildende höhere Schule*, AHS), lower and upper secondary vocational schools (*Berufsbildende mittlere und höhere Schule*, BMHS) pre-vocational schools (*Polytechnische Schule*, PTS), part-time vocational schools of the dual system (*Berufsschule*, BS) and special-needs schools (*Sonderschule*, ASO). Number of schools are approximate values due to overlapping school types in some cases.

Figure 5.11. School sizes across school types

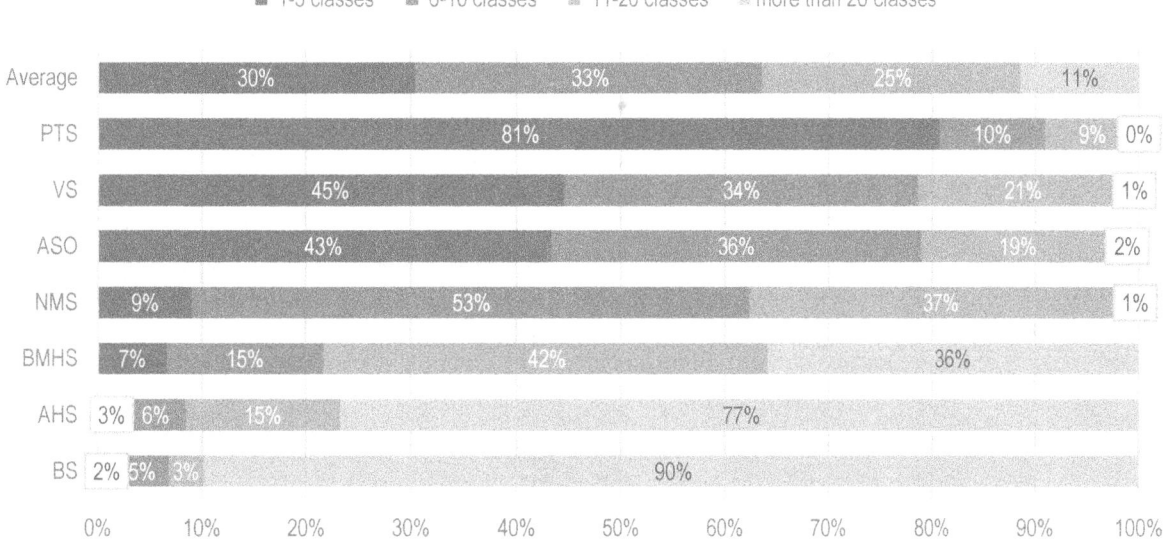

Note: N=2651. School type abbreviations refer to primary schools (*Volksschule*, VS), lower secondary schools (*Neue Mittelschule*, NMS), upper secondary general education schools (*Allgemein bildende höhere Schule*, AHS), lower and upper secondary vocational schools (*Berufsbildende mittlere und höhere Schule*, BMHS) pre-vocational schools (*Polytechnische Schule*, PTS), part-time vocational schools of the dual system (*Berufsschule*, BS) and special-needs schools (*Sonderschule*, ASO).

Table 5.3. School leader response rates across provinces

Province	Number of schools	Share of all schools	Responses	Response rate
Burgenland	275	6%	161	59%
Carinthia	389	7%	175	45%
Lower Austria	1232	18%	470	38%
Upper Austria	1021	21%	545	53%
Salzburg	382	6%	163	43%
Styria	844	13%	333	39%
Tyrol	631	12%	318	50%
Vorarlberg	291	4%	119	41%
Vienna	680	14%	367	54%
Overall	**5745**	**100%**	**2651**	**47%**

Source: Own data, BMBWF (2017[6]), *Zahlenspiegel 2017: Statistiken im Bereich Schule und Erwachsenenbildung in Österreich [Statistical data 2017: Statistics in the area of school and adult education in Austria]*, Bundesministerium für Bildung Wissenschaft und Forschung (BMBWF), Vienna, https://bildung.bmbwf.gv.at/schulen/bw/ueberblick/grunddaten.html.

In the survey, most school leaders have between two and ten years of professional experience in their current position. More than a third of (38%) of school leaders have more than 10 years of professional experience. In contrast, only 15% state that they have less than two years of professional experience.

Of the 2 651 school leaders who completed the survey, 264 took the opportunity to provide additional comments in the last question. The most commonly raised concern (25%, 66 out of 264) is that school leaders often do not have enough time and resources (such as organisational staff for administrative tasks) to prepare and use evidence. Other common barriers brought forward pertain to a lack of practice-oriented preparation of evidence, and a shortage of guidance to use evidence (16%, 41 and 42 out of 264 respectively). 14% of school leaders who responded to the question, highlighted that evidence for them pertains not only to quantitative data, in particular results from standardised tests, but also to qualitative evidence. 14% wish for additional/ other offers of evidence to support school leaders, while 6% of responses highlight a lack of common understanding of evidence to hinder the evidence use. Furthermore, 13% expressed their wish for more exchange, both with colleagues but also with different levels of decision-making in the education system (Figure 5.12).

Figure 5.12. Barriers to use evidence expressed in school leaders' additional responses

Note: Common themes among responses to question "Are there any further suggestions/ innovative examples from your professional experience of using evidence?" Multiple themes in one response possible. N=**264**. Category 'other remarks' includes issues such as too high formality/standardisation, culture and staff related issues, administrative hierarchy.

Schools developing the skills to use evidence for autonomous quality development

School leaders require the individual skills to access and make sense of evidence. This pertains to the skills to locate, appraise, and synthesise evidence and integrate it with other information and particular needs. This can include identifying relevant evidence sources for their school, such as new studies, and the cooperation with university colleges of teacher education and other research institutions. It also includes identifying and adapting useful parts of available evidence for the needs of their specific school context. Importantly, school leaders also should be able to guide and instruct teachers and other staff in their school to build the skills to use evidence effectively in their daily work. This includes school leaders' building the respective skills as well as being able to rely on resources helping them guide and instruct the use of evidence by their staff.

> *School leaders emphasise the need for own initiative to acquire skills relevant to using evidence. Collegial exchange is the main source for schools leaders in this respect.*

Most commonly, school leaders learn from other colleagues about how to access and make sense of evidence. Overall, eight in ten schools leaders report that they acquire skills for evidence use through exchanging with colleagues. Slightly less widespread are training courses with seven out of ten school leaders reporting respective opportunities available to them. Mentoring and coaching as well as e-learning solutions are less common. More than half of the 61 school leaders who provided additional remarks on this issue, highlighted the need for self-initiative to acquire skills for evidence use. This includes own initiative in finding relevant literature and material, finding and paying for private coaching, and cooperating with a private institution.

There are notable differences between school types. Virtually all other school types (between 88% and 97%) report at least some opportunity to acquire skills relevant to access and make sense of evidence. However, almost a third of school leaders in schools of the vocational dual system (BS) report that they do not see any possibilities to acquire such skills. Moreover, in these schools only six in ten school leaders report to exchange with colleagues to build respective skills.

Beyond being able to use evidence individually to help them develop the quality at their school, school leaders should have the skills to guide and instruct the use of evidence by school staff. Close to seven in ten school leaders report opportunities to acquire these skills through training courses. However, only a third reports so with respect to trainings tailored to the supervisory capacity of school leaders. Four in ten school leaders report that they can rely on advisory services to help them guide and instruct the use of evidence by teaching staff. This includes in particular *Rückmeldemoderatoren/-innen* (feedback moderators)[4]. Moreover, about a quarter of school leaders reports access to mentoring or coaching offers with the aim to promote skills to use evidence. Opportunities to build respective skills through e-learning solutions, such as learning platforms, are less common (17%). Vorarlberg presents a provincial outlier. Here, a third of schools leaders report not to have any suitable opportunity in this respect, more than twice than in other provinces.

Of the 56 school leaders who provided additional remarks, 60% highlight the need of self-initiative or emphasise the importance of collegial exchange to acquire the skills to guide and instruct the use of evidence of school staff. Factors arising from school leaders' professional context are a specific concern in acquiring the skills to use evidence for decisions at the school level and instructing and guiding the use of evidence by teachers. As one school leader highlights:

> "As [school leader] of a small school with a high teaching commitment, I would be very happy if seminars and other support services for [school leaders] were offered in the afternoon/ weekends. Almost all seminars [...] are full-day offers. However, I cannot attend a seminar in the morning as I have to teach in the morning [...]."

Organisational resources support school leaders to instruct and guide teaching staff to use evidence in their practice as well as acquire respective skills. This includes education and training requirements for teaching staff, instructions for conducting reflection discussions, and the possibility to initiate professional development measures helping teaching staff to build the skills to use evidence (Langer, Tripney and Gough, 2016[2]; Gray et al., 2012[3]). Guidelines and advice related to reflection and planning discussions with teaching staff can help school leaders to encourage teachers' use of evidence. Staff development measures allow school leaders to refer to regulations that require teachers to pursue professional development in how to use evidence for decision-making. Other examples mentioned to help school leaders to guide and instruct the use of evidence at their school are the quality management system for general education and associated methods and tools for systematic quality assurance (*Schulqualität Allgemeinbildung*, SQA), the SAND tool[5], and reviews of education standards (*Bildungsstandards-Überprüfung*, BIST-Ü). About half of school leaders report that they can rely on education and training requirements to encourage teachers to acquire the skills to use evidence. Four in ten school leaders report they can rely on guidelines for teacher reflection discussions and have professional development measures for teachers at their disposal.

Making evidence conveniently available to schools

Evidence needs to be communicated and conveniently accessible, to increase its use in school leaders' decision-making. Evidence can be communicated directly, for example through newsletters, publications, handouts, research teasers or research summaries. Evidence providers may make evidence available also through other means of access, such as through databases or evidence repositories.

> *Schools make greatest use of evidence gathered at the school level and rely on quality development staff and school quality managers for support*

The vast majority of school leaders produce and use school-level evidence from standardised student testing (82%) and internal evaluations (87%). This includes in particular, reviews of education standards (*Bildungsstandards-Überprüfung*, BIST-Ü) and standardised graduation and diploma examination results (*Standardisierte Reife und Diplom Prüfung*, SRDP/SRP); evidence gathered through tools and methods aligned to quality management systems (SQA and QIBB, respectively)[6]; and results from diagnostic tools, such as informal competence assessment (*Informelle Kompetenzmessung*, IKM). More than half of school leaders who completed the survey, report to engage with research evidence to update and create new knowledge. A large majority of school leaders (84%) reports that school staff prepares evidence themselves.

Many school leaders took the opportunity of the survey to provide additional comments on what kind of evidence they prepare for their school. Examples include self-prepared statistical evidence within schools, such as school-developed competency catalogues, competence checks via the school's own learning platform, annual student and teacher surveys and statistical information of registration and graduate numbers. Many examples pertain to qualitative evidence. This includes regular and intensive discussions with the teaching staff at the school, feedback from students and parents tailored to the school, and networking with school-leader peers. Moreover, some school leaders also provided examples of successful collaborations with universities. One example is a cooperation between a school and the University of Vienna's Centre for Teacher Education, which helps choosing annual evaluations on varying topics that the school picks to make progress in school development. At the intersection between acquiring skills using evidence effectively and accessing evidence, six in ten school leaders frequently or regularly work with quality development staff (SQA/QIBB) to support use of evidence in their school. Around 50% of school leaders report that they work frequently or regularly with school quality managers/ school supervision to support them in using evidence effectively. However, this is subject to pronounced provincial differences (Figure 5.13).

Figure 5.13. Schools working with school quality managers to support use of evidence

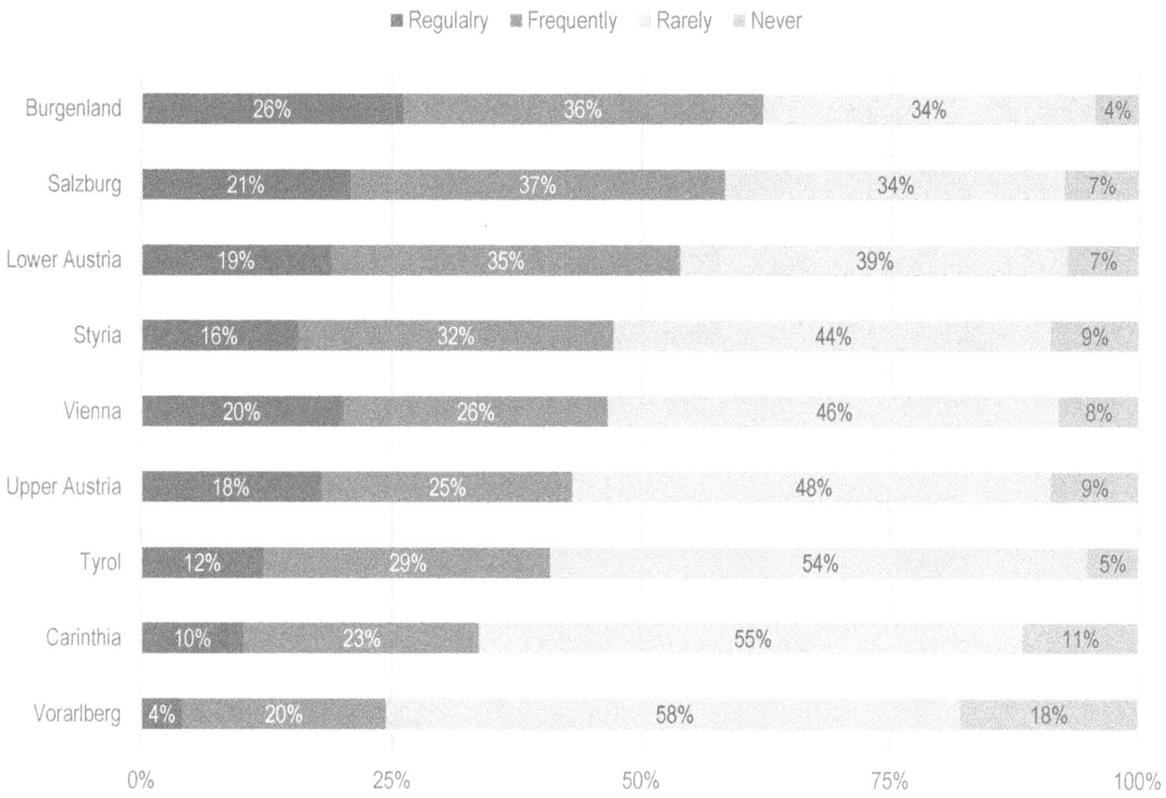

■ Regulary ■ Frequently ■ Rarely ■ Never

Region	Regularly	Frequently	Rarely	Never
Burgenland	26%	36%	34%	4%
Salzburg	21%	37%	34%	7%
Lower Austria	19%	35%	39%	7%
Styria	16%	32%	44%	9%
Vienna	20%	26%	46%	8%
Upper Austria	18%	25%	48%	9%
Tyrol	12%	29%	54%	5%
Carinthia	10%	23%	55%	11%
Vorarlberg	4%	20%	58%	18%

Note: N=2651. Answer to question "How often do you use the listed facilities to support you in the effective use of evidence? [school supervision]" Multiple answers possible.

Feedback moderators (*Rückmeldemoderatoren/-innen, RMM*) help schools to process, analyse and interpret results from reviews of education standards (*Bildungsstandards-Überprüfung*, BIST-Ü). Practical support of subsequent school and instructional development processes is the task of school development advisory services (*Entwicklungsberatung in Schulen*, EBIS), a support initiative within SQA. Contrary to the widespread use of school-internal support and the work with school quality managers, three-quarters of schools rarely or never consult external advisory services, such as EBIS and quality process managers at the federal or provincial level (*Bundes-qualitätsprozessmanager/-innen*, BQPM; *Landes-qualitätsprozessmanager/-innen*, LQPM). Similarly, 85% of schools rarely or never consult feedback moderators (RMM) to support them in the effective use of (specific) evidence (Figure 5.14). Of the 264 school leaders who provided additional comments, over 25% highlight that they have capacity issues preventing them to prepare and use evidence. Especially in primary education (*Volksschule*), school leaders identify teaching responsibilities and a lack of administrative staff as bottlenecks for systematic evidence use.

Figure 5.14. Schools work with selected support offers to help them use evidence effectively

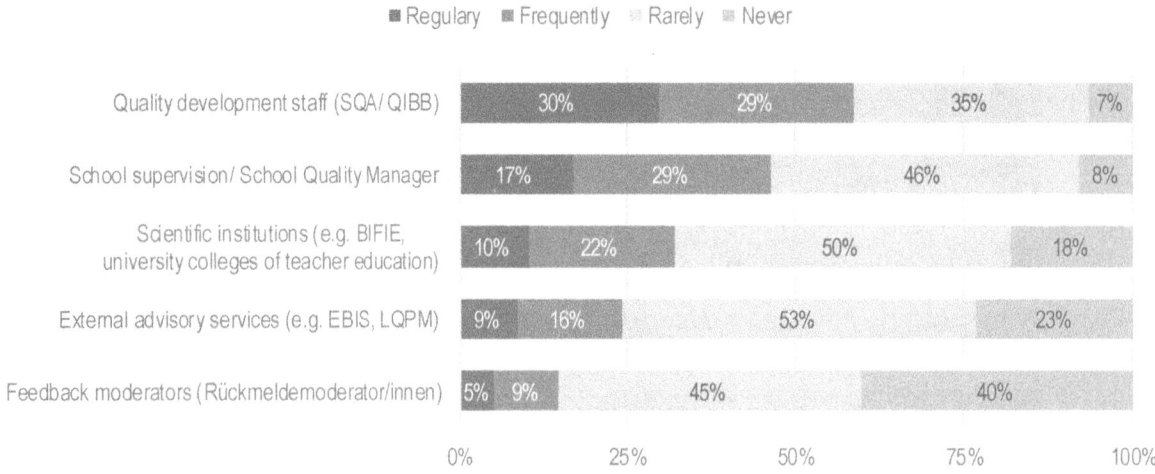

Note: N=2651. Answer to question "How often do you use the listed facilities to support you in the effective use of evidence? Multiple answers possible.

Schools' impressions are mixed regarding externally provided evidence. School leaders wish for greater involvement to help tailor provided evidence to their context

While useful to some, others do not consider evidence provided by the BMBWF as prepared in a user-friendly manner. Overall, only 41% of school leaders consider the BMBWF/ education directorates as largely or always interested in providing schools with evidence that is user-friendly. However, another 40% of school leaders considers this to be the case little or not at all. This differs by school type. Over half of school leaders of upper secondary schools (AHS) and half of school leaders at schools for secondary and higher vocational education (BMHS) report positively when asked about user-friendly preparation of evidence provided by the BMBWF. In contrast, only 30% of school leaders of pre-vocational schools (PTS) report positively. On average, school leaders report evidence provided by research institutions, such as BIFIE and university colleges of teacher education, overall as more usefully prepared for their needs.

A minority of school leaders report that evidence providers appear to consider different experiences in dealing with evidence (25%) and different interests in topics (35%) to tailor evidence to the needs arising from work processes and context of school leaders. The tailoring of evidence based on language needs is infrequently observed by school leaders (9%). Moreover, close to 15% of the 264 additional comments highlight a lack of user-friendliness or practice-orientation. As one school leader illustrates,

> "Evidence should be more user-friendly. I understand the intention to present surveys as scientifically as possible (e.g. language use), but this makes them difficult to use. If one has to read through such evidence (explanations) several times to understand their purpose and sense, one will not fall back on such evidence knowledge in the future."

A number of school leaders identify concrete measures to help them make better use of evidence in their specific context. This includes tools for evidence-based work through SQA; evaluation tools adaptable to specific projects or locations (tools previously used may not be available anymore (e.g. *Tevalo*) because of new data privacy regulations (DSGVO); evidence repository from which schools could autonomously choose what to use and through which (primary) schools can access site-specific evidence points.

Consulting schools and school leaders in making evidence available provides an opportunity for evidence providers to shape communication techniques, modes of access and presentation of evidence in a manner that is most relevant for schools' needs. For instance, school leaders may be invited to give feedback on the content and communication of certain types of evidence, or to contribute content by sharing practices from their local context. On average, over a third of school leaders report that school leaders are not involved in the provision and communication of evidence (28% feel unable to assess this). Where school leaders are consulted, they report this to be the case mainly within evaluations (23%). Other forms are very rare, such as consultation on relevant topics, contributing to content, improving communication channels or type of preparation.

There are notable differences across school types in how involved school leaders feel specifically regarding consultation on relevant topics of external evidence. Almost a third of schools for secondary and higher vocational education (BMHS) (27%) report that school leaders are consulted about the topics relevant to them, but only 8% of school leaders at pre-vocational schools (PTS) report so. In comparison, 16-20% of school leaders from all other school types report so.

Organisational processes to encourage evidence use in schools

Organisational processes and structures can encourage schools to use evidence and reduce respective barriers. For schools, this includes making decisions and decision-making processes plain, such as exchanging with external stakeholders and school partners. It also includes inviting diverse perspectives in different areas of decision making, for example through processes of shared leadership. Moreover, knowledge management systems help contextualise evidence to develop actionable knowledge. Such systems include online platforms and databases, as well as offline collections, for instance in the form of printed handbooks, organisational documents, or teaching materials.

Schools focus on internal exchange over involvement with external partners to increase clarity around decisions and decision-making processes.

Schools' efforts to make transparent how decisions were reached emphasise the exchange among teachers. Overall, nine out of ten school leaders use exchange formats with teachers to clarify decisions and processes. The observation is uniform across school types and school sizes. Around four in ten school leaders engage in exchange externally with school partners to increase clarity around decisions and their decisions-making processes. This is relatively more popular among very large schools (with more than 20 classes) and among upper secondary vocational and general education schools (*Allgemeine höhere Schule*, AHS; *Berufsbildende mittlere und höhere Schule*, BMHS).

Overall, a quarter of schools makes use of (publicly available) documents to make decisions and decision making processes transparent and comprehensible. Vocational schools put relatively more emphasis on this particular measure than general education schools (Figure 5.15). A number of school leaders took the opportunity to share examples of how their school seeks to increase clarity around school decisions and processes. This includes inter-school student councils and approaches of democratic leadership in the school.

Figure 5.15. School's efforts to clarify decisions and how decisions are reached

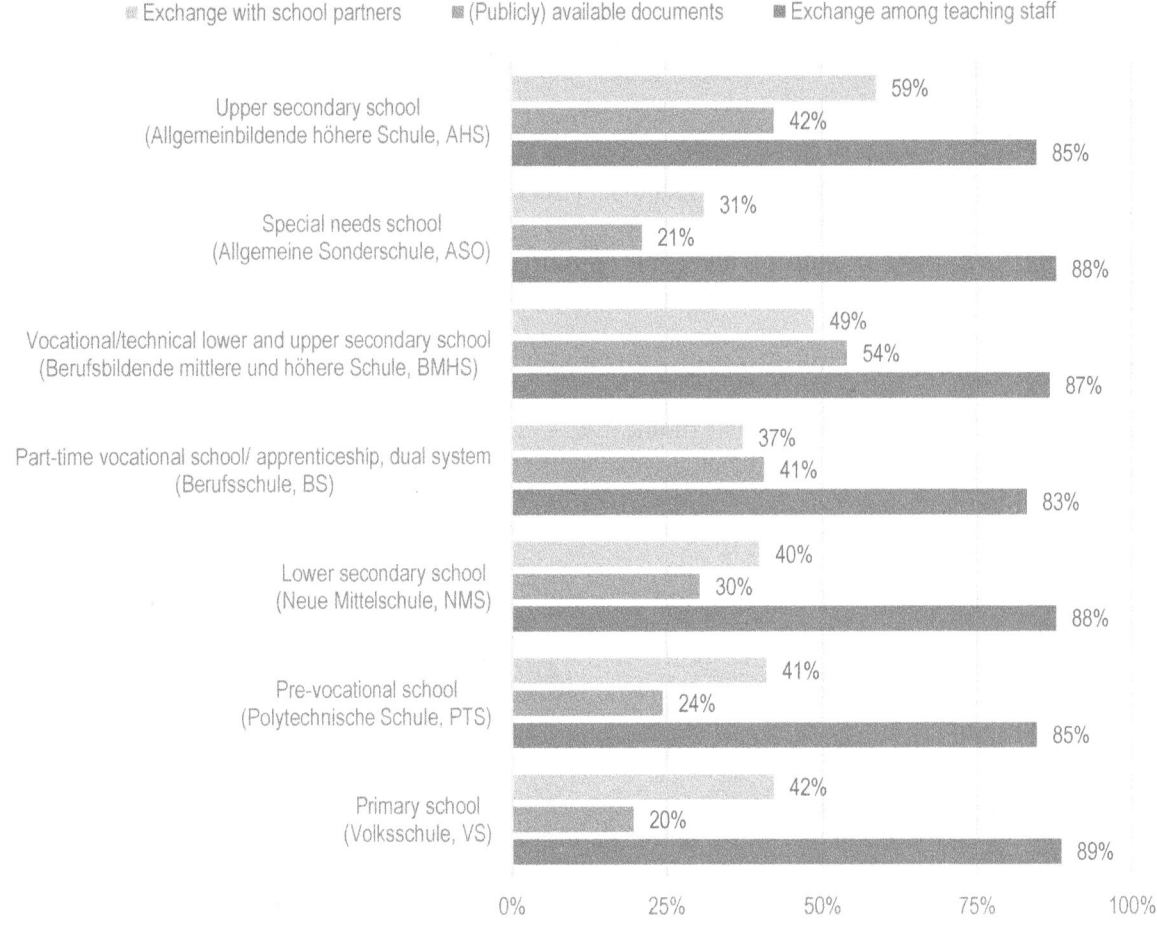

Note: N=2651. Answers to question "Are there efforts to make decision-making processes at your school clear and comprehensible?" Multiple answers possible.

Schools involve diverse perspectives mainly to help develop classroom teaching but vocational and special-needs schools also emphasise staff development

Around three-quarters of school leaders often or regularly involve different perspectives in decisions. This includes perspectives of parents, students, teachers, as well as external school partners. Overall, efforts to include diverse perspectives in developing classroom teaching are most common (73%). Decisions around organisational development (66%) are less common. Decisions regarding staff development (62%) are the least frequent.

Larger schools have a slight tendency to involve diverse perspectives more often. In particular, very large schools emphasise involving diverse perspectives in organisational development over developing classroom teaching. Accordingly, upper secondary general education schools (AHS) (75% have over 20 classes) and part-time vocational schools (BS) (90% have over 20 classes) frequently involve diverse perspectives in organisational development. Notably, vocational schools (BS, BMHS) and special-needs schools (ASO), emphasise involving different perspectives in staff development compared to other school types (Figure 5.16).

Figure 5.16. Schools involve diverse perspectives mainly in development of classroom teaching

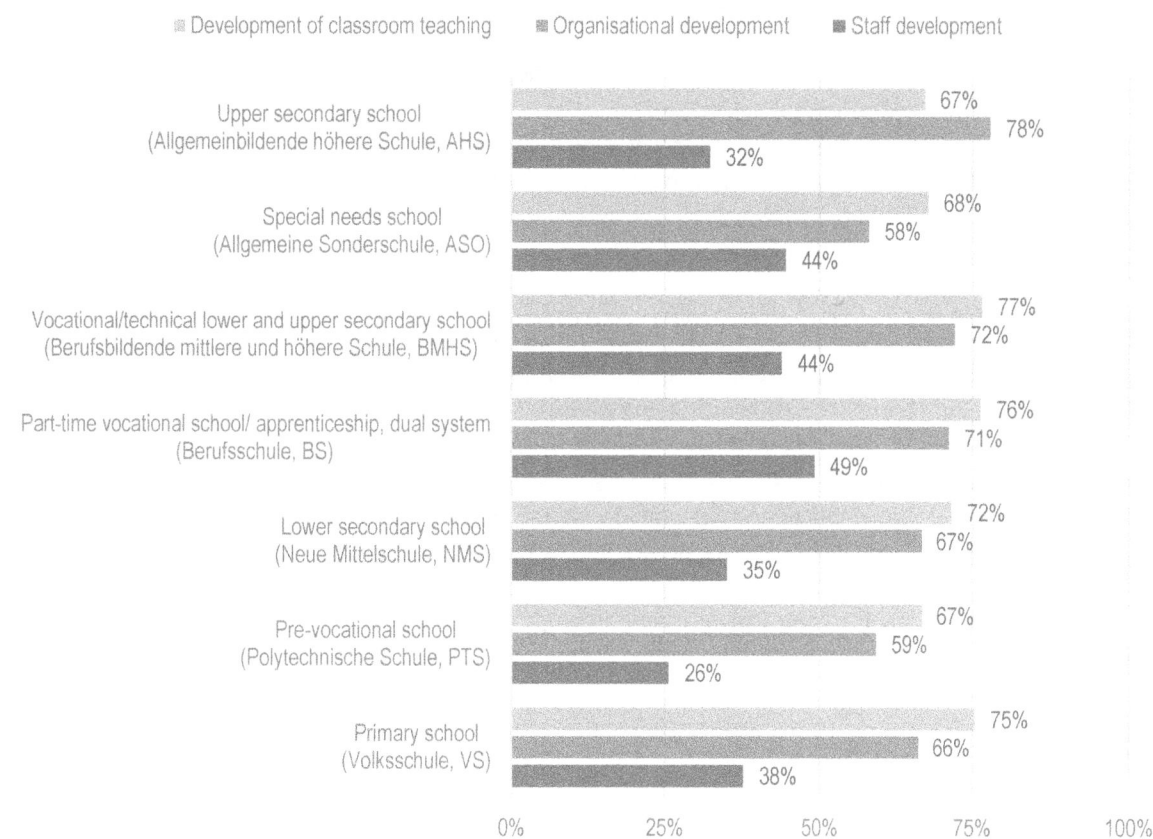

N=2651. Answers to question "In which processes at your school are different perspectives (e.g. parents, teachers, students) involved in decision-making?" Multiple answers possible.

Schools are not systematically aware of knowledge management systems

Knowledge management systems link knowledge across and within organisations for access by decision makers where needed. By doing so, they help contextualise evidence. This can include general information management, a collection of organisational procedures, or other knowledge relevant to the functioning of the organisation and the decision-making processes at hand. Today, knowledge management systems are often computer-based but likewise include printed material. Individual school leaders may have clear ideas of the information to which they wish access in form of a knowledge management system, making it worthwhile to consult them in making available respective systems.

Two-thirds of school leaders report that school staff can rely on internal knowledge management systems to organise and share knowledge within the individual school. This is particularly the case in vocational schools (BMHS, 72%; BS, 75%), but less the case in pre-vocational schools (PTS) (53%). Knowledge management systems that allow organising and linking knowledge across the Education Region varies across provinces. In Burgenland and Tyrol, 58% and 44% of schools report to use regional knowledge management systems, while only a quarter of schools in Vienna, Vorarlberg, Styria and Carinthia report to do so. To make best use of knowledge management systems, respective systems should be available to all decision makers and all decision makers should be aware of available systems. However, school leaders appear to lack a common understanding of knowledge management systems. Among others, school leaders identify school supervision, training and support offers as knowledge management systems.

Schools' exchange with evidence providers and exchange among school leaders

An important aspect to promote the systematic use of evidence in schools is to build trusted relationships and facilitate social influence through interaction with those who are engaged in evidence production and experienced in using evidence. Accordingly, central to fostering the use of evidence is facilitating and encouraging the exchange among schools and schools' exchange with providers of evidence. In Austria, providers of evidence are for example the federal ministry, education directorates, the national institute for education research (*Bundesinstitut für Bildungsforschung, Innovation & Entwicklung*, BIFIE), university colleges of teacher education (*Pedagogische Hochschulen*, PH) and other organisations such as the national statistics bureau Statistik Austria.

School leaders exchange with evidence providers but organisational support may be lacking

Overall, about four in ten school leaders report they engage in a structured exchange with evidence providers at least once a year. There are notable differences between provinces and school types. Over 50% of school leaders in secondary general education (AHS, NMS) and vocational schooling (BMHS) engage in such exchanges. Special-needs schools (ASO), pre-vocational schools (PTS) and part-time vocational schooling of the dual (apprenticeship-combined) system (BS) engage less frequently. Around seven in ten schools of these school types do not regularly engage in structured exchange with evidence providers. About eight in ten schools that exchange with evidence providers report that this is at least most of the time carried out to improve the preparation or quality of evidence. School leaders report less frequently (50%) adequate organisational support of such exchanges, for instance, through time or human resources.

Figure 5.17. Schools' exchange with evidence providers

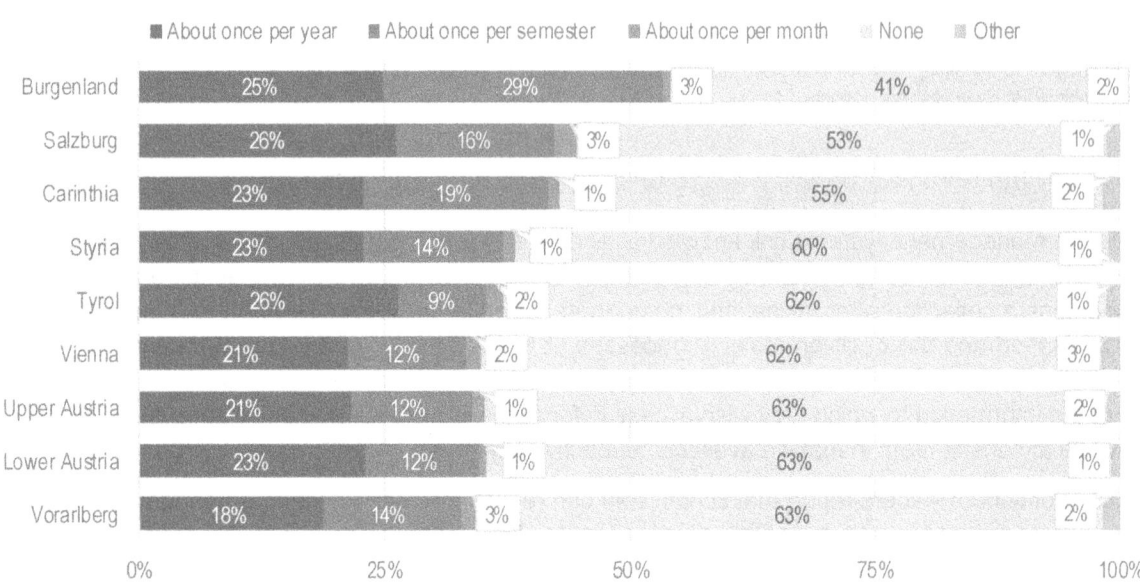

Note: N=2651. Answers to question "Is there a structured exchange between the providers of evidence (e.g. BIFIE, university colleges of teacher education) and you as a decision maker at the school?"

Schools in Burgenland stand out as exchanging with evidence providers particularly frequently. Here, three in ten Schools exchange with evidence providers about once per semester (Figure 5.17). Schools in Burgenland and Salzburg further report greater organisational support to carry out these exchanges. Here, about two-thirds of school leaders report organisational resources to be most of the time or always available to support them, compared to half of school leaders overall (Figure 5.18).

Figure 5.18. Organisational support of school's exchange with evidence providers

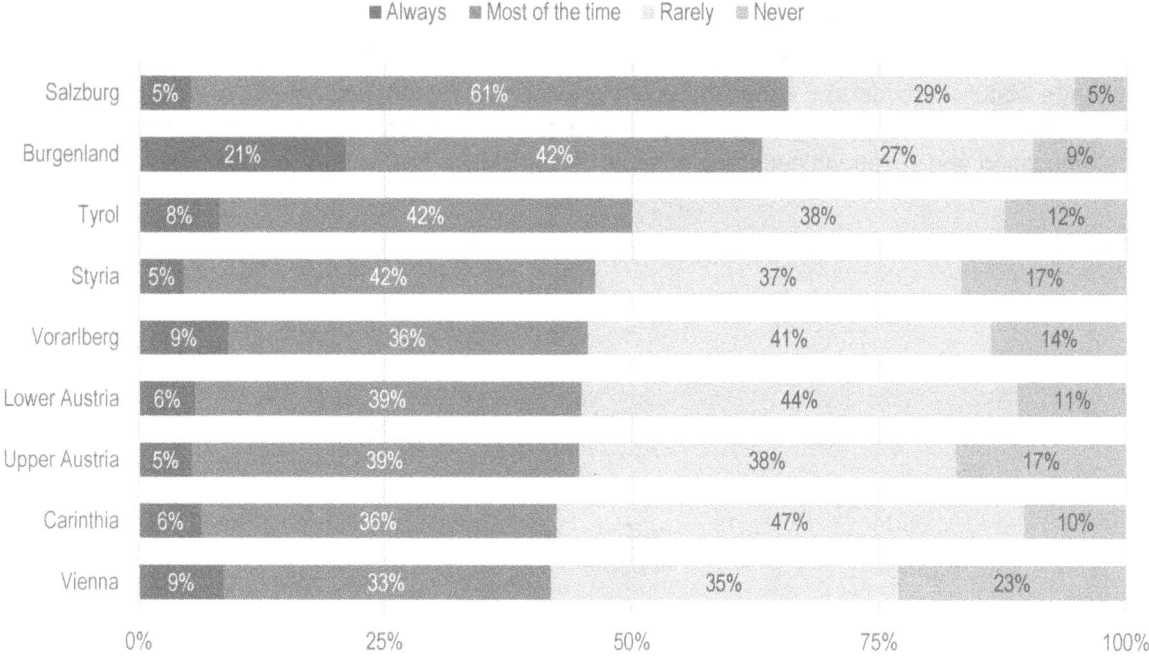

Note: Follow-up question drawing on positive responses to question "Is there a structured exchange between the providers of evidence (e.g. BIFIE, PH) and you as a decision maker at the school?" Answer to question "The exchange is supported organisationally (e.g. in terms of time/staff resources)". N=**1064**.

School leaders, who provided additional comments on their exchange with evidence providers highlighted that they exchange as necessary, but not regularly. According to these comments, typical occasions for such an exchange on demand are school supervision, performance review and objective-setting discussion (*Bilanz- und Zielvereinbarungsgespräche*, BZG), within informal competence checks (*Informelle Kompetenzmessung*, IKM) or, formerly, education standards review (*Bildungsstandards-Überprüfung*, BIST-Ü), within the project *securing basic competencies* (*Grundkompetenzen absichern*, GRUKO) and in school-based professional development (*Schulinterne Fort- und Weiterbildung*, SCHILF). Performance review and objective-setting discussions (BZG) are part of SQA and QIBB. They regularly take place between managers of adjacent levels of governance and are based on the current development plan of the subordinate level.

School leaders frequently exchange with colleagues informally and in work meetings regarding methods and experiences of using evidence

Overall, nine in ten school leaders exchange with colleagues regarding methods and experiences related to using evidence in schools' quality development. Discussion of evidence is carried out predominantly informal and frequently takes places within work meetings, rather than institutionalised, for instance through dedicated network meetings. As other opportunities to exchange with colleagues, school leaders further identify the (discontinued) Leadership Academy (LEA)[7], SQA, and events within school-based professional development (SCHILF).

There is high variation across provinces and across school types in how systematically school leaders discuss evidence in collegial exchange. School leaders in Burgenland, Salzburg, and Styria report systemically to exchange with each other about using evidence in their practice, with only 2-7% of school leaders reporting no exchange with colleagues (Figure 5.19). Within these exchanges, they discuss research findings, reviews of education standards (*Bildungsstandards-Überprüfung, BIST-Ü*), or standardised students test results (SDRP) more systematically than their colleagues in other provinces. There are notable differences across different school types. Around 20% of school leaders at vocational schools of the dual (apprenticeship-combined) system (*Berufsschule*, BS) never engage with colleagues to exchange about methods and experiences using evidence. School leaders of pre-vocational schools report similarly little exchange with colleagues. In contrast, 10% school leaders in primary and secondary general education and vocational/technical schools (AHS, BMHS, NMS and VS) report so.

Figure 5.19. School leaders' collegial exchange on methods and experiences using evidence

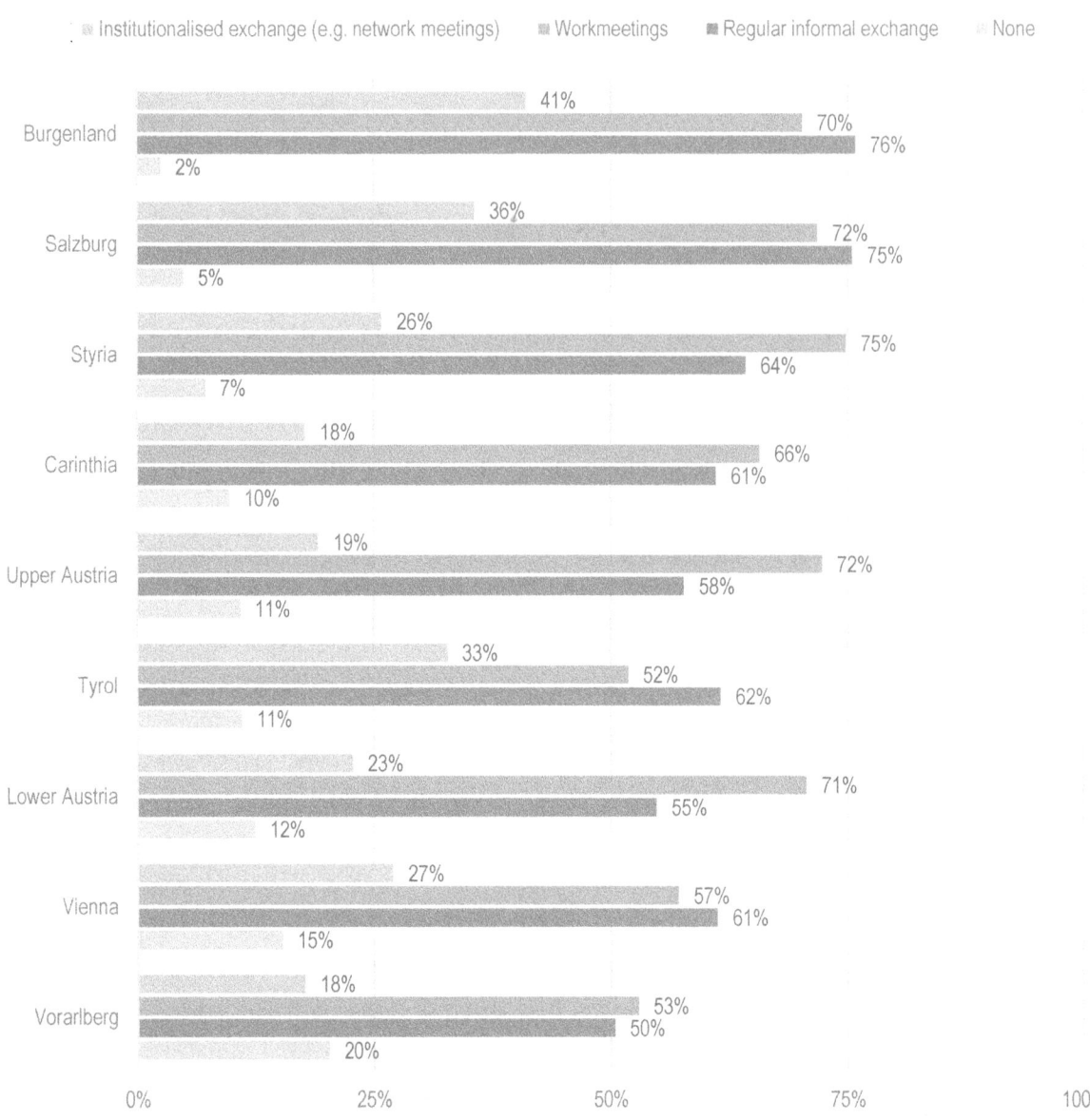

Note: N=2651. Answer to question "Are there opportunities specifically to exchange with colleagues about experiences and methods of using evidence?" Multiple answers possible.

Raising awareness of evidence and developing a common understanding how to use it

To promote the use of evidence for decision making in schools, school leaders and teaching staff need to be mindful of evidence use as a principle of good decision making. Schools need to adjust to greater autonomy and potentially new areas of decision making. Central to using evidence for new or changed responsibilities depends centrally on developing a shared understanding of what constitutes fit-for-purpose evidence, and how evidence should be used best in specific situations of decision making, such as decisions about developing classroom teaching or school development. Important elements to raise awareness include events and advisory services, information and training material. School leaders additionally mention informal exchanges, work meetings, printed material and events related to SQA and pedagogical conferences as means to develop awareness for the merits and importance of using evidence in day-to-day decisions as well as for strategic quality development.

Half of the school leaders who completed the survey, report the use of information material to raise awareness of the use of evidence as a basis for decision making at the school. One-fifth of schools report such efforts through consulting or events offered by education directorates and the BMBWF. Across school types, 44% of pre-vocational schools report that there are no efforts at the school to raise awareness. In contrast, the share of school leaders without any means at their disposal to raise respective awareness amounts to 25% to 35% among other school types. More than half of school leaders report efforts at their school to develop a common understanding of how to use evidence in concrete decision-making situations within school development and development of classroom teaching. A minority of schools report such efforts in staff development (20%) and organisational processes (35%). As one school leader illustrates,

> *"All measures concerning evidence use are currently only carried out by me as the school leader. There is probably still a long way to go to create an understanding of evidence use, so that it becomes practically apparent that very valuable development processes can arise from it."*

Close to nine in ten school leaders report efforts to create a common understanding of what constitutes fit-for-purpose evidence for specific decision-making challenges. A notable difference is Vorarlberg, where a quarter of school leaders report no such efforts, compared to under 15% of school leaders across other provinces. Efforts to build a common understanding of what constitutes fit-for-purpose evidence as well as how evidence should be used in specific decision-making areas include discussions of standardised graduation and diploma examination results (*Standardisierte Reife und Diplom Prüfung*, SRDP/SRP), school-based professional development (*Schulinterne Fort- und Weiterbildung*, SCHILF), meetings, conferences and joint discussions on the review of education standards (*Bildungsstandards-Überprüfung*, BIST-Ü).

References

BMBWF (2019), *Steuerung des Schulsystems in Österreich: Weissbuch [Governance of the Education System in Austria: White Paper]*, Bundesministerium für Bildung, Wissenschaft und Forschung, Abt. III/3, http://www.bmbwf.gv.at. [1]

BMBWF (2017), *Zahlenspiegel 2017: Statistiken im Bereich Schule und Erwachsenenbildung in Österreich [Statistical data 2017: Statistics in the area of school and adult education in Austria]*, Bundesministerium für Bildung Wissenschaft und Forschung (BMBWF), Vienna, https://bildung.bmbwf.gv.at/schulen/bw/ueberblick/grunddaten.html. [6]

Burns, T., F. Köster and M. Fuster (2016), *Education Governance in Action: Lessons from Case Studies*, Educational Research and Innovation, OECD Publishing, Paris, https://dx.doi.org/10.1787/9789264262829-en. [4]

Gray, M. et al. (2012), "Implementing evidence-based practice", *Research on Social Work Practice*, Vol. 23/2, pp. 157-166, http://dx.doi.org/10.1177/1049731512467072. [3]

Langer, L., J. Tripney and D. Gough (2016), *The Science of Using Science - Researching the Use of Research Evidence in Decision-Making*, EPPI-Centre, Social Science Research Unit, UCL Institute of Education, University College London, http://eppi.ioe.ac.uk/cms/Default. (accessed on 15 January 2018). [2]

Shewbridge, C. and F. Köster (2019), *Strategic Education Governance - Project Plan and Organisational Framework*, http://www.oecd.org/education/ceri/SEG-Project-Plan-org-framework.pdf. [5]

Notes

[1] The Federal Institute for Educational Research, Innovation and Development (*Bundesinstitut für Bildungsforschung, Innovation und Entwicklung des österreichischen Schulwesens*, BIFIE) has since been restructured to form the Institute of the Federal Government for Quality Assurance in the Austrian School System (*Institut des Bundes für Qualitätssicherung im österreichischen Schulwesen*, IQS). The change took effect on 1 July 2020.

[2] In addition, results of external school evaluation (when implemented) are set to be essential evidence that will form a basis for individual schools' quality development.

[3] In Vorarlberg, two School Quality Managers feel they cannot assess whether they are adequately involved. This may be related to the little time in this position. In Vorarlberg, 50% of the eight SQMs who have completed the survey have less than 2 years of experience in this role, compared to ca. 12% across all provinces.

[4] School leaders can request feedback moderators (*Rückmeldemoderatoren/-innen*) via the university colleges of teacher education. Feedback moderators advise schools on the analysis and interpretation of the results of the education-standard reviews and support them in processing the results. School leaders and teaching staff initiate and see through the subsequent school and instructional development processes.

[5] The Federal Institute for Educational Research, Innovation and Development (BIFIE) offers the SAND as tool for school development. The tool allows analysing and comparing data individual and across school locations.

[6] SQA and QIBB are the respective quality management systems for general education (*Schulqualität Allgemeinbildung*, SQA) and vocational education and training (*QualitätsInitiative BerufsBildung*, QIBB). Both systems include tools and methods for systematic quality assurance. With the 2017 governance reform they are superseded by a quality management system common to all schools.

[7] The Leadership Academy (LEA) network comprised decision makers across levels and areas of the Austrian education system who participated in seminars over the course of one year. LEA seminars were carried out between 2004 and 2018.

6 Conclusions and outlook

This section describes overarching key findings, identifies relative strengths and weaknesses across five areas to promote use of evidence, and develops possible next steps for Austria to pursue.

An important aspect of the 2017 governance reform in Austria is to strengthen the use of evidence for decision making at all levels of governance to accompany the changes in responsibilities, specifically those of schools and school supervision (school quality managers). To this end, Austria partnered with the OECD Strategic Education Governance project to take stock of efforts promoting the systematic use of evidence in the Austrian education system. The following sections highlight overarching key findings and identify the relative strengths and weaknesses over five areas to promote use of evidence. Finally, the chapter provides an outlook on possible next steps.

This report sought to offer an indication of well-developed areas to promote the systematic use of evidence and areas with room for improvement. Carried out as an online survey to decision makers in the federal ministry, education directorates, school supervision and school leaders, it is meant as a "thermometer" gauging areas for further investigation and informing thinking about possible next practices. It is designed as a conversation starter rather than a definitive evaluation of practices. Following the spirit of a self-reflective exercise, the report is set to inform discussions at a workshop with stakeholders of all levels of governance in the Austrian education systems.

Overarching key findings

The report indicates that some provinces engage in efforts to promote the use of evidence highly systematically. In these provinces, school quality managers consistently report to exchange frequently with colleagues and with evidence providers to improve quality and preparation of evidence. Across schools, school leaders systematically report to exchange with school quality managers and to exchange with peers about methods and experiences to work with evidence. They report systematically that their exchanges are supported organisationally, such as through requisite time or staff resources. In other provinces, such efforts are emergent. For instance, some schools and school quality managers engage frequently in exchanges to improve quality and preparation of evidence; others do less so with reports of a lack of organisational support for exchanges being more frequent.

School quality managers play a pivotal role in fostering the use of evidence. They see room to be more involved in the provision and preparation of evidence. More than 90% of school quality managers engage in efforts to raise awareness of the merit and importance of using evidence in decision making. While there is a clear focus on working with school leaders to build awareness in schools, six in ten school quality managers also engage teaching staff in schools directly. While school quality managers are largely content with the evidence that is available, they express motivation to be more involved in preparing and providing evidence. They seek greater interaction with key providers of evidence.

Schools have some key organisational processes in place that can encourage the use of evidence in decision making. Approaches that promote transparency in decisions taken and how they were reached can motivate the use of evidence. School leader reports show an emphasis on internal exchange to increase clarity around school decisions and decision-making processes. Inviting a range of perspectives, experiences, and knowledge into different areas of decision-making can strengthen systematic use of evidence by motivating consideration of different sources of evidence. School leaders mainly report inviting diverse perspectives, for instance from teachers, parents, and students, to help develop classroom teaching. However, vocational and special-needs schools moreover underscore this approach also for staff development decisions.

Schools are important evidence producers. The vast majority of school leaders produce and use school-level evidence from internal evaluations (87%) and standardised student testing (82%). Many school leaders (84%) report that school staff prepares evidence themselves, which reflects the comparatively widespread use of teacher-developed tests in Austria as found by PISA (OECD, 2016[1]). Results have uncovered many concrete examples of evidence preparation at the school level. Many school leaders took the opportunity of the survey to highlight their school-level efforts of preparing evidence, which can provide a starting point to further dialogue and investigation. Examples include self-prepared statistical evidence within schools, such as school-developed competency catalogues, competence checks via the school's own learning platform, annual student and teacher surveys and statistical information of registration and graduate numbers. Moreover, many examples referred to efforts to gather additional qualitative evidence. Examples included regular and intensive discussions with the teaching staff at the school, feedback from students and parents tailored to the school, and school leaders networking with peers. Some school leaders also provided examples of successful collaborations with universities.

Evidence provided to schools is not always adequately prepared for them and their work environment. Only half of all school quality managers who participated in the survey report that the preparation of evidence for schools is largely (42%) or very (8%) adequate. Shortcomings in the user-friendliness and practice-orientation of evidence with which schools are provided is a recurring topic among responses of school leaders. School leaders consider the BMBWF/ Education directorates as less concerned with preparing the evidence they provide to schools in a user-friendly way than other evidence providers. Among school leaders only a minority (41%) considers the BMBWF/ education directorates as largely or very interested in providing evidence in a user-friendly way; 43% of school leaders consider this to be the case little or not at all. Conversely, 56% of school leaders consider research institutions for the most part or very concerned with preparing evidence for schools in a user-friendly manner.

Relative strengths and weaknesses over five areas to promote use of evidence

The online survey among executives at the BMBWF and education directorates, school quality managers, and schools leaders gathered multifaceted insights about the present opportunities and efforts carried out that research finds to promote the opportunity, capability and motivation to use evidence effectively and systematically. The survey covers five areas to promote the systematic use of evidence areas:

1. The skills to access and makes sense of evidence.
2. Making evidence conveniently available.
3. Organisational processes encouraging the use of evidence.
4. Collaboration with evidence producers and collegial exchange.
5. Building a common understanding of the importance of evidence, which evidence is useful and how its best used in specific situations.

Questions gathered information about the type of efforts and solicited additional information about the context and practices. A look at those questions that can be divided into positive and negative answers allows for an indication of relative strengths and weaknesses across the different areas.

The responses among school leaders and school quality mangers point towards **relative strengths** in terms of present opportunities and efforts in two areas (Figure 6.1). First, in the area of developing skills to access and makes sense of evidence, on average around eight in ten school leaders give positive responses. Within this area, school leaders answer particularly positive regarding opportunities to develop skills to access and make sense of evidence (nine out of ten school leaders). Also for school quality managers, opportunities to develop skills around using evidence are well established albeit on a lower level (85% positive responses among school leaders, 77% positive responses among school quality mangers). The main barrier to more a positive picture in this area is a perception among school quality managers of fewer opportunities to build skills to guide and instruct the use of evidence among schools (seven out of ten school quality managers answer positively) (Figure 6.2).

Figure 6.1. Relative strong and weak areas to promote the systematic use of evidence

Aggregated share of positive responses among school leaders and school quality managers for each area

Note: see Figure 6.2 for positive responses to individual questions used to calculate averages in the areas of: the skills to access and makes sense of evidence (Skills), making evidence conveniently available (Availability), organisational processes encouraging the use of evidence (Organisational processes), collaboration with evidence producers and collegial exchange (Interaction), and building a common understanding of the importance of evidence, which evidence is useful and how its best used (Standards). Any response other than none/no/never is counted as positive. Questions with no negative answer options (no/none/never) are omitted.

A second area of strength among school leaders and school quality managers pertains to developing evidence-use as a principle of good decision-making and developing common understanding of how to use evidence (Figure 6.1). In this area, around eight in ten school leaders and school quality managers answer positively to questions in this area, albeit with different emphases. Close to nine in ten school leaders report efforts to develop common understanding in the school on how evidence should be used and to develop a common understanding which evidence is fit-for-purpose in specific decision-making challenges. However, only seven in ten school leaders report efforts to build awareness for use of evidence as principle of good decision-making. From the responses emerges a picture that school quality managers emphasise building awareness for use of evidence as a principle of good decision-making and efforts to develop a common understanding on how evidence should be used. Less frequently reported are efforts to develop a common understanding which evidence is fit-for-purpose in specific decision-making situations (Figure 6.2).

Out of the five areas to promote the systematic use of evidence, making evidence conveniently available is a **relatively weak area** with around six out of ten school leaders and school quality managers responding positively to questions in this area (Figure 6.1). The area covers the topics whether provided evidence is perceived as well-targeted and user-friendly, and whether the users feel adequately involved. Among school leaders, user-friendliness of evidence provided to schools by the federal ministry and education directorates particularly leaves room for improvement (four in ten school leaders answer positively). User-friendliness of evidence provided by research institutions is reported more favourably with overall around six in ten school leaders answering positively. While school leaders feel overall adequately involved in making evidence available (six in ten), only three in ten school quality managers regard their involvement in making evidence available favourably (Figure 6.2).

Figure 6.2. Overview of positive responses across areas to promote systematic use of evidence

Share of positive responses among school leaders and school quality managers per area

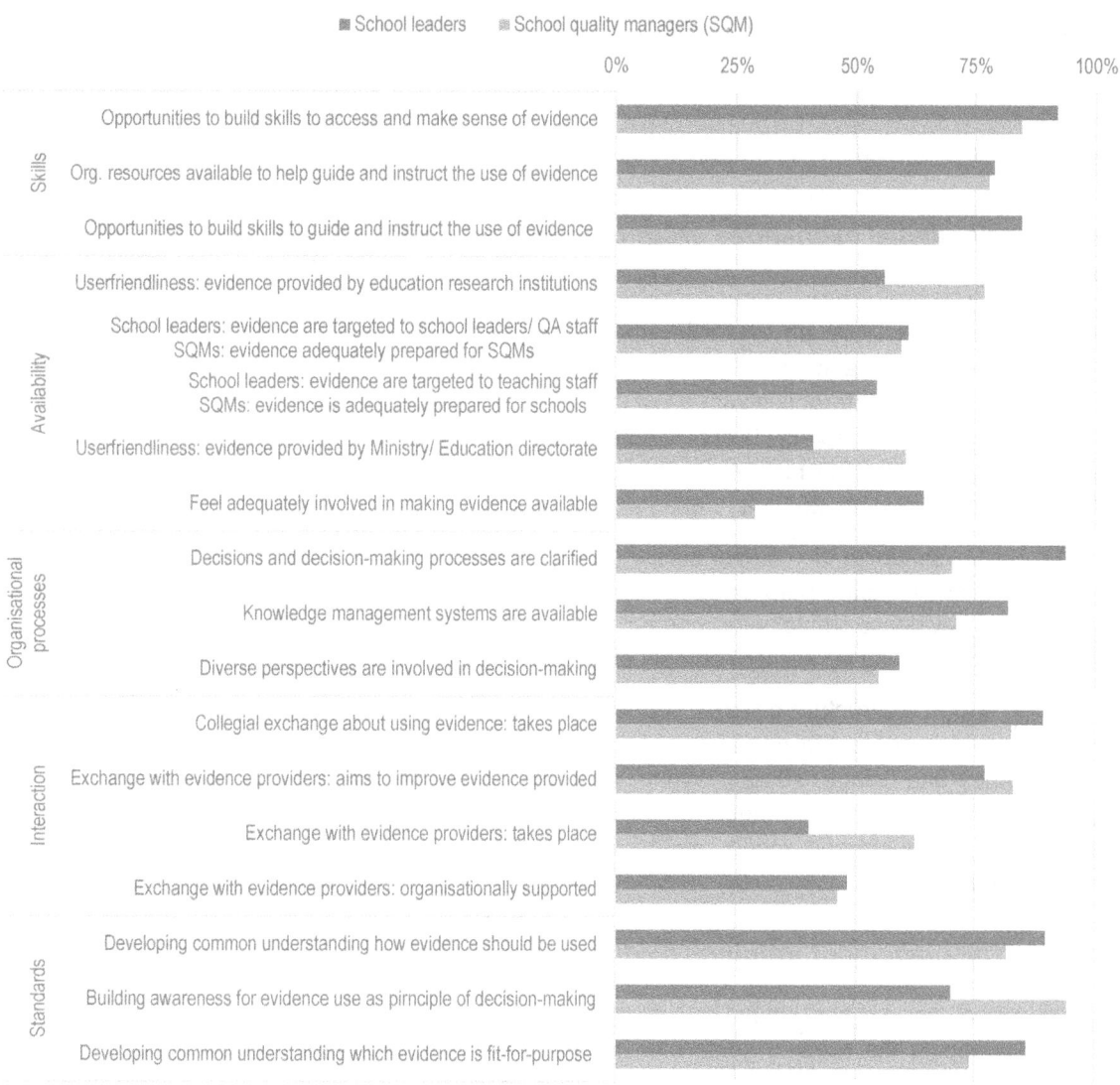

Note: Any response other than no/none/never is counted as positive. Questions with no negative answer options (no/none/never) are omitted. Ordered by decreasing share of positive answers within each area (average of school leaders and school quality managers).

For the areas of interaction and organisational processes, the responses show a more mixed picture. The area of interaction includes exchanges among colleagues and the exchange with evidence providers. Overall, six in ten school leaders report favourable opportunities within this area – however, while structured exchanges with colleagues are very widespread (eight in ten school quality managers and nine in ten school leaders report positively), only four in ten school leaders report exchanges with evidence providers. However, where school leaders do exchange with evidence providers, these exchanges are frequently aimed at improving provided evidence. Whereas school quality managers exchange substantially more frequently with evidence providers (six in ten) than school leaders, among both school leaders and school quality managers organisational support is reported favourably by only half of respondents. In the area of organisational processes, the analysis highlights very encouraging responses regarding school leaders' efforts to clarify decision and how these decisions were reached, with around nine in ten school leaders reporting such practices overall. Among school quality managers, the adoption of such practice indicates some room for improvement. However, school quality managers' responses show very widespread engagement in building awareness for the merits of evidence use for decision-making (nine in ten school quality managers engage in respective efforts). Inviting diverse perspectives in decision-making is overall a less employed practice both within schools and among school quality mangers (Figure 6.2).

Possible next steps

Structuring collegial exchanges around explicit purposes taking into account already existing habits

Interactions with peers are an important channel for school leaders and school quality managers to exchange experiences and methods around using evidence. Empirical research emphasises the advantages of frequent interaction with a low threshold to interact, for instance in collegial exchange, over more ambitious, but (necessarily) less frequent interactions on the one hand and the benefits of structured exchange around an explicit purpose on the other (Shippee et al., 2013[2]; Langer, Tripney and Gough, 2016[3]; O'Mara-Eves et al., 2013[4]).

To maximise the potential of collegial exchanges to promote the use of evidence, exchanges should be structured around an explicit purpose to this end. Purposes include developing skills to gather, access and make sense of evidence, developing common understanding of what makes evidence fit for a specific purpose, and developing agreement on how evidence should be used in a specific situation.

Importantly, efforts to structure collegial exchanges should take current habits and processes as point of departure to avoid burdening decision makers and increase their adoption (Bunn and Sworn, 2011[5]; Langer, Tripney and Gough, 2016[3]). Where decision makers already engage systematically in relevant efforts, efforts to structure exchanges further can be counter-productive. Specifically, in some provinces school quality managers and school leaders already engage in efforts to promote the use of evidence highly systematically.

Increasing availability of trainings to develop skills to guide and instruct evidence use

For both school leaders and school quality managers, strengthening their evidence-related capabilities includes developing the skills to guide and instruct the use of evidence in schools. Yet, availability of respective trainings is reported comparatively infrequently. For both school leaders and school quality managers, exchange among peers is one of the main sources to strengthen evidence-related skills. Increasing the availability of trainings specifically aimed at fostering skills to guide and instruct the use of evidence can help promote use of evidence directly and insert important new knowledge into collegial exchanges to this end.

Supporting school leaders and school quality managers develop a common understanding around using evidence

The 2017 reform changed responsibilities of school quality managers and schools. Developing a common understanding around using evidence pertains to developing agreement around which evidence is fit-for-purpose for which tasks and how it is best used in concrete situations. This is particularly relevant in the transition to new responsibilities as specific decision-making situations and habits are still emerging.

With the reform, schools received greater autonomy, particular in terms of staff decisions and developing school quality. In this respect, developing a common understanding of using evidence includes determining which evidence is fit for purpose for specific responsibilities, such as staff development, and how and when is this most useful. School quality managers may take a role here in facilitating exchange across school types. For instance, responses show that special-needs schools (*Sonderschule,* ASO) engage more frequently in efforts to include diverse perspectives in staff decisions than primary schools, which are comparable in average number of classes. The BMBWF and education directorates can take a role in supporting schools and school quality managers in developing standards around using evidence. This includes facilitating exchanges between school quality managers and schools, as well as exchanges of school quality managers and schools with other evidence providers. Exchanges should be structured around explicit purposes; taking into account already existing habits and processes.

Collaboratively reflecting on which evidence is best gathered where

While schools are important evidence producers, in some circumstances others (e.g. school quality managers) will be in a better position to gather and prepare fit-for-purpose evidence. Similarly, some evidence may be best prepared and contextualised by research institutions, such as the IQS[1]. In the same vein, schools will be in a better position to gather evidence needed at other levels, for instance, by school quality managers to optimise the regional education offer. Different levels of governance – in particular, school leaders and school quality managers – should be involved in this reflection as decision-making situations and challenges are still emerging in light of changed responsibilities.

Improving tailoring of and user-friendly access to evidence through exchange with decision makers

Not all decision makers will be equally prepared to gather and prepare evidence as needed for their new responsibilities. Encouraging evidence providers to tailor evidence to the habits and capacities of decision makers – for instance to the needs of school leaders with less routine in using evidence – can help bring everyone along in the transition to new responsibilities. Tailoring evidence can support decision makers adjust to changed responsibilities and respective demands on using evidence. Making fit-for-purpose evidence available in a user-friendly way reduces burden for decision makers and increases take-up of evidence sources.

Tailoring of evidence and providing user-friendly access to evidence depends on information about decision makers' work processes and habits. Evidence providers may gather respective information through exchanges with decision makers. Responses indicate that school quality managers are motivated to be directly involved in preparing evidence, while low-threshold information exchanges may be more suitable when soliciting schools' input (Figure 6.2).

References

Bunn, F. and K. Sworn (2011), "Strategies to promote the impact of systematic reviews on healthcare policy: A systematic review of the literature", *Evidence & Policy: A Journal of Research, Debate and Practice*, Vol. 7/4, pp. 403-428, http://dx.doi.org/10.1332/174426411X603434. [5]

Langer, L., J. Tripney and D. Gough (2016), *The Science of Using Science - Researching the Use of Research Evidence in Decision-Making*, EPPI-Centre, Social Science Research Unit, UCL Institute of Education, University College London, http://eppi.ioe.ac.uk/cms/Default. (accessed on 15 January 2018). [3]

O'Mara-Eves, A. et al. (2013), "Community engagement to reduce inequalities in health: A systematic review, meta-analysis and economic analysis", *Public Health Research*, Vol. 1/4, pp. 1-526, http://dx.doi.org/10.3310/phr01040. [4]

OECD (2016), *PISA 2015 Results (Volume II): Policies and Practices for Successful Schools*, PISA, OECD Publishing, Paris, https://dx.doi.org/10.1787/9789264267510-en. [1]

Shippee, N. et al. (2013), "Patient and service user engagement in research: A systematic review and synthesized framework", *Health Expectations*, Vol. 18/5, pp. 1151-1166, http://dx.doi.org/10.1111/hex.12090. [2]

Note

[1] The Institute of the Federal Government for Quality Assurance in the Austrian School System (IQS) superseded the Federal Institute for Educational Research, Innovation and Development of the Austrian School System (BIFIE). The change took effect on 1 July 2020.

Annex A. Glossary

Shorthand	Full name (English name)	Description
BIFIE	Bundesinstitut für Bildungsforschung, Innovation und Entwicklung des österreichischen Schulwesens (Federal Institute for Educational Research, Innovation and Development of the Austrian School System)	The aim of BIFIE is to plan, implement and evaluate effective quality assurance and development measures. Core tasks include educational monitoring, a national education report, quality development and applied educational research. **N.B.** The BIFIE has been restructured to form the Institute of the Federal Government for Quality Assurance in the Austrian School System (*Institut des Bundes für Qualitätssicherung im österreichischen Schulwesen*, →IQS). The change took effect on 1 July 2020.
BIST BIST-Ü	Bildungsstandards (BIST) (Education standards) Bildungsstandards-Überprüfung (Education standards review)	Until 2018/19, education standards were reviewed within the framework of the BIST-Ü Bildungsstandards-Überprüfung (Education standards review). Education standards will continue to form the basis of the instrument of informal competence assessment (*Informelle Kompetenzmessung*, →IKM), which will be continued and expanded as a national performance measurement.
BZG	Bilanz- und Zielvereinbarungsgespräche (Performance review and objective-setting discussions)	Development plans at all levels and performance review and objective-setting discussions (*Bilanz- und Zielvereinbarungsgespräche*, BZG) between the different levels of the school system represented the two central structural elements of the →SQA framework. Development plans are accompanied by regular performance review and objective-setting discussions (BZG) between the decision makers at superordinate levels, which are based on the current development plan of the subordinate level. A number of support measures are available for implementation, including training courses, information material (e.g. via the website), external consultants and SQA coordinators at school and provincial level.
EBIS (SQA)	Entwicklungsberatung in Schulen (School Development Advisory Services)	The wide range of support measures for the implementation of →SQA at each individual school also includes the EBIS initiative. The aim of EBIS is to ensure and further develop the quality of external support and advice for schools in their development processes.
eVOCATION	eVOCATION (n/a)	The eVOCATION institute offers further education and training for individual teachers, for teaching staff or project groups, as well as support for schools in the area of talent, achievement and potential development. It is based on a comprehensive pedagogical concept.

GruKo	Grundkompetenzen absichern (Securing basic competencies)	GruKo deals with compulsory schools whose students have failed to meet at least 20% of the education standards in the education standards reviews and whose school results are below their expected value. The universities of teacher education prepare special offers for the participating schools. Together with the school management or the teaching staff, multi-professional teams (usually consisting of school developers, subject didacticians and school psychologists) analyse the reasons for the below-average performance at the respective school and provide individually tailored support and advice over several years.
IKM	Informelle Kompetenzmessung (Informal competence assessment)	With IKM, the →BIFIE provides teachers with a tool for evaluating their own teaching in primary, secondary and lower secondary schools, which provides simple, reliable and free information about the learning level of the whole class or group as well as the level of competence of each individual pupil.
IQS	Institut des Bundes für Qualitätssicherung im österreichischen Schulwesen (Federal Institute for Quality Assurance in the Austrian School System)	The IQS was established on 1 July 2020 to promote the effective and practical use of data and evidence for quality assurance processes in the Austrian school system previously collected by →BIFIE. The IQS is a subordinate agency of the BMBWF. The expertise and infrastructure of BIFIE have been transferred.
LEA	*Leadership Academy* (n/a)	The Leadership Academy (LEA) network was composed of managers at all levels of the Austrian education system (managers of all school types, school supervision, education administration and pedagogy), who participated in fourteen one-year training courses from 2004 to 2018.
QPM (QIBB) SQPM LQPM BQPM	(Schul-/ Landes-/ Bundes-) QualitätsProzessManager/in ((School-/ Provincial-/ Federal-) Quality Process Manager)	Quality process managers have distributed responsibility for operational tasks supporting the implementation of →QIBB at school, provicial and federal level (school quality process managers SQPM, province quality process managers LQPM, federal quality process managers BQPM)
QIBB	QualitätsInitiative BerufsBildung (Quality Initiative Vocational Education and Training)	Since 2004, QIBB has been the strategy of the BMBWF for implementing systematic quality management in the Austrian school system for Vocational Education and Training (VET).
RMM	Rückmeldemoderation (Feedback moderation)	School leaders can request feedback moderators (RMM) via the universities of teacher education. They advise schools on the analysis and interpretation of results of the standard reviews and support them in the fact-based processing of these results. The concrete formulation and implementation is then carried out by school leaders and teachers. The practical support of subsequent school and instructional development processes is not the responsibility of feedback moderators; it is the task of trained school and instructional development consultants (→EBIS).

SAND (Tool)	SAND - Schulentwicklung durch Analyse und Nutzung von Daten (School development through analysis and use of data)	In addition to the documents made available, →BIFIE offers a support tool for school supervision to accompany the development of schools. SAND (or SanD^{BIST}) enables the data of all school locations in the area of responsibility to be analysed together and compared.
SCHILF	Schulinterne Fort- und Weiterbildung (school-based professional development)	SCHILF pertains to school-based professional development. Depending on the target group these may be offered for the teaching staff of one school, one region, one province or several or all provinces.
Schule im Aufbruch	*Schule im Aufbruch* (School on the move)	*Schule im Aufbruch* is a platform that calls on all stakeholders within schools to share experiences and examples, and to encourage each other to take the next steps towards better child development in schools.
SLS	*Salzburger Lesescreening* (Salzburg reading screening)	SLS allows teachers to check quickly the reading ability of students. It is available free-of-charge to Austrian schools teaching 6 to 14-year-olds and is provided by the Federal Ministry for Education Science and Research under a general public licence. It has been compulsory in the third and fifth grades since the 2004/05 school year.
Sokrates	*Sokrates* (n/a)	*Sokrates* is an administrative software and knowledge management system for schools. It allows management of information around students, teachers and general school administration. Through the software, schools transmit specific data to the Austrian National Statistics Office (Statistik Austria)
SQA	Schulqualität Allgemeinbildung (School quality General education)	SQA (*Schulqualität Allgemeinbildung*) is a system for pedagogical quality development and quality assurance in general education. SQA pertains to methods and tools for decision makers at all levels of the school system to improve processes and results. SQA pools resources, provides support and creates structures and binding procedures for quality development. It also comprises elements to build awareness for quality development.
SRDP/SRP	Standardisierte Reife und Diplom Prüfung (Standardised Graduation and Diploma Examination)	The Standardised Graduation and Diploma Examination (*Standardisierte Reife und Diplom Prüfung*, SRP/SRDP) is designed to assess student performance objectively, transparently and fairly. It comprises three independent sub-areas to assess students' competencies at the end of upper secondary education: The pre-scientific thesis at general education upper secondary schools (*Allgemeine höhere Schule*, AHS) or diploma thesis (*Berufbildende höhere Schule*, BHS), two or three oral examinations, and three or four written examinations. The performance assessment in the written part is carried out by the subject teacher using standardised correction and assessment instructions. Otherwise, the exercises continue to be prepared by the teachers at the school location.

www.ingramcontent.com/pod-product-compliance
Lightning Source LLC
Chambersburg PA
CBHW080554170426
43195CB00016B/2784